vel E

Finish Line
Writing

Continental Press
Elizabethtown, PA 17022

Credits

Writing, Editorial, Design, and Production by Brown Publishing Network, Inc.

Illustrators: Pages 16, 19, 25, 28, 45, 50, 78, 97, 112, 113, 114, Carol O'Malia; Pages 29, 30, 31, 36, 41, 51, 55, 62, 72, 84, 98, 105, Ruth Flanigan.

Photo Credits: Front cover and title page: top, © 2005 www.indexopen.com/Index Stock Imagery; bottom left, Copyright Dynamic Graphics, CREATAS brand Royalty Free; bottom right, Copyright BananaStock Ltd. All rights reserved.; background, Photograph by Kendall Walker; Page 2, © 2005 www.indexopen.com/Index Stock Imagery; Page 14, © 2005 www.indexopen.com/Index Stock Imagery; Page 24, © 2005 www.photospin.com; Page 28, © 2005 www.indexopen.com/Index Stock Imagery; Page 35, Lori Adamski Peek/Getty Images; Page 46, Paula Bronstein/Getty Images; Page 56, *Declaration of Independence*, © 2005 www.photospin.com; *Benjamin Franklin signature*, webexhibits.org; *Thomas Jefferson signature*, www.vmi.edu/archives; Pages 61, 65, © 2005 www.indexopen.com/Index Stock Imagery; Page 92, Julian Wasser/Getty Images; Page 100, © 2005 www.photospin.com; Page 108, Steve Parry/Monsoon/PictureQuest; Page 120, Joseph Devenney/Getty Images.

ISBN 978-0-8454-4865-6

Copyright © 2006 The Continental Press, Inc.

No part of this publication may be reproduced in any form or by any means, electronic, mechanical, photocopying, recording, or otherwise, without the prior written permission of the publisher. All rights reserved. Printed in the United States of America.

Contents

Introduction 2

Lesson 1
The Writing Process 4

Lesson 2
Writing a Paragraph 14

Lesson 3
Writing Sentences 22

Lesson 4
Main Idea and Details 30

Lesson 5
Cause and Effect 40

Lesson 6
Comparison and Contrast 50

Lesson 7
Opinions and Facts 60

Lesson 8
Writing Sentences 70

Lesson 9
Writing a Narrative 80

Lesson 10
Informational Writing 88

Lesson 11
Descriptive Writing 96

Lesson 12
Writing to Persuade 104

Lesson 13
Writing Sentences 112

Test-taking Tips 122
Practice Test 123
Handbook 128
Proofreading Symbols .... Inside back cover

Welcome to Finish Line Writing

Do you think of yourself as a writer? You are! And you probably know a lot about writing. You know that it takes hard work and creative thinking. You know that sometimes writing can take many days. Your teacher probably encourages you to work carefully to make your writing successful. You may also write at home—perhaps letters or e-mails—on topics you choose.

But not all writing is the same. When you take a writing test, for example, your time is limited. Often you cannot choose your own topic. You need to be able to make a plan and organize your ideas quickly. This special kind of writing—test writing—is different from the writing you do at school or at home. In order to do well on test writing, you need to learn some strategies. This book will give you tips for doing well on writing tests.

Test writing is not totally different from your regular writing. Take a look at some ways that test writing and classroom or at-home writing are alike.

- **process approach**—No piece of writing comes out perfect the first time. Writers use these steps to create a quality piece of writing—prewriting, drafting, revising, and proofreading.

- **clear main idea**—Whether writing for science, a local newspaper, or a state achievement test, writers must clearly focus on a topic or main idea so readers are not confused about the writer's primary purpose.

- **support for ideas**—Details and examples are two important ways to support a main idea. If writers want readers to believe what they have written, they must provide evidence or support for their ideas.

- **strong organization**—A few good ideas sprinkled throughout a piece of writing are not helpful to a reader if the rest of the writing is disorganized. Writers must put sentences and paragraphs in an order that helps readers understand the main idea.

How is test writing different from classroom writing?

In test writing, you must complete the assignment within a shorter period of time. If you had more time, you might do the writing differently. However, it is important for you to write for the test as completely as possible. Even with the time constraint, you should rely on the steps of the writing process to write for a test. To help you remember the steps clearly, think of the shorter version that you will find throughout this book: Plan, Write, Edit, Check.

Strategies for Test Writing

You can use the following strategies to prepare to write quickly and completely on writing tests:

- **Identify what the writing question is asking for.** Look for the main idea in the writing question. What does the assignment ask you to do? In this book you will learn to answer different types of writing questions. You will write using cause and effect, comparison and contrast, and opinions and facts. You will also write using narrative, informational, descriptive, and persuasive formats.

- **Know the language.** Your response will be stronger if you are familiar with some of the language in test writing. In *Finish Line Writing*, you will learn to read assignment questions for several types of writing.

- **Stay focused.** When you are writing a story or a report in school, you are using writing to explore your ideas. You might let your imagination wander. But when you are writing for a test, you must stay focused on only what the writing task requires. For example, if you are assigned to write a description, you should not get off track writing your opinion.

- **Skip your own experience.** When you write for school or pleasure, you often draw on your own experiences in life. In writing tests, you need to focus on what the question asks. Test writing is primarily intended to see if you can respond in writing to a specific question, often about something you will read.

Now you are ready to use this book. When you finish, you should be familiar with the structure of writing tests.

You will also be able to

- recognize different types of writing questions,
- know where to start and what to look for in a writing question,
- apply specific skills and approaches to the various writing questions, and
- feel confident that you can write well on any test!

Lesson 1 — The Writing Process

Writing is a process—something you do in steps. Most writers follow these four steps:

1 Prewriting
2 Drafting
3 Revising
4 Proofreading

An easy way to remember the writing process is to think of what you do in each step. In the prewriting step, you **plan** what you will write. The drafting step is when you actually **write**. After that, you go back for the revising step. This means that you **edit** what you have written. Finally you proofread, or **check**, your writing.

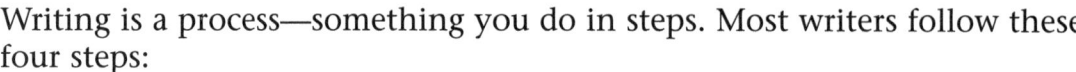

1 Prewriting

In the prewriting step, you plan what you will write. To start, you need to think about the following:

- Why you are writing (your purpose)
- What you will write about (your subject)
- What you will say (the content)
- How you will say it (your voice)
- Who will read it (your audience)

Sometimes, however, you are writing for a test. Then, some of these things are already decided for you. For example, read this question from a test.

> Robots like C-3PO and R2-D2 in the *Star Wars* movies are very different from the robots that exist in real life today. Write an article for your school newspaper that compares and contrasts the robots of science fiction movies with real robots.
>
> In your article, be sure to include
> - how science fiction robots and real robots are similar
> - how they are different

This question tells you the purpose (to compare and contrast), the subject (robots), and the audience (the students in your school). The rest is up to you. You need to work out the content—what information you will present and how you will organize that information. Many writers begin by jotting down notes.

Graphic Organizers

Sometimes it helps to use a graphic organizer when you are planning your writing. For this assignment, you might use a comparison and contrast chart like this one.

Prewriting

Robots
What's Different?

Movies	Real Life
• They look and act more like humans than machines.	• They look more like machines than humans.
• They are programmed to do things like translate languages and deliver secret plans.	• They do work that is boring or dangerous.
• They can be loyal friends.	• They don't really have feelings or emotions.
• C-3PO has "creativity circuits," which allow him to tell stories.	• They have artificial intelligence, so they can do things like move around objects and pick things up.

What's the Same?
They are mechanical devices.
They are designed to do work that is usually done by humans.
They replace humans in certain kinds of jobs.

For different types of writing, other graphic organizers, like these, may be helpful.

- **Cluster map or web** – This organizer can help you get your ideas on paper for many kinds of writing.

- **Venn diagram** – A Venn diagram can help you organize your ideas when you want to compare and contrast two things.

- **Sequence chart** – A sequence chart is best when you are writing a narrative. It helps you map out events in the order they happen.

Finish Line Writing 5

2 Drafting

After you have worked out your plan, it's time to put your ideas into sentences and paragraphs. This step is **drafting**. Don't worry about spelling and grammar at this point. You can change things later. The important thing now is to write down your ideas.

There are two ways to draft what you want to write. One is just to start writing, letting your ideas move forward. This works well for some writing tasks. You can write as you think about what you want to say. But you will probably need to spend a lot of time revising what you have written.

The other way is to work from the prewriting plan you made. Here is a draft that could be written based on the comparison and contrast chart on page 5.

> **Drafting**
>
> Robots in movies look and act more like humans then machines. Real robots look more like machines then humans. R2-D2 and c-3PO, the robots in the Star Wars movies, have lots of human characteristics. They feel loyal, and form friendships. They do things like translate langauges and deliver secret plans. R2-D2 can only beep and whistle. C-3PO even has creativity circuits that enable him to make up stories.
>
> The real robots we have today are more like smart machines. They have artificial intelligence and can do jobs in factories. They do dangerous work like handling toxic materials and defusing bombs. You can buy a robot vacuum cleaner. It's a flat oval machine that moves over the floor. It senses where dirt is and goes there to suck it up. When its done, it goes back to it's base.
>
> The robots in sci-fi movies and real robots have some things in common They do work that is normally done by humans and can replace humans in certain kinds of jobs.

3 Revising

Once you have finished drafting, the next step is **revising**. In this step, you read what you have written and make changes to improve your work. You edit your writing so that it will be clear to your readers.

When you revise, you might need to change the content of your work, or you might revise its structure. Asking yourself these questions can help you decide what changes you should make to improve what you have written.

Content
- Does my writing have a main idea?
- Have I included enough supporting details?
- Is there any place where I should add an important detail or example?
- Have I included details that are not important and should come out?
- Does my writing have an introduction and a conclusion?

Structure
- Is my writing organized in a way that fits the topic?
- Are the relationships between my ideas clear?
- Do I need to add words, phrases, or sentences to make them clearer?
- Do my sentences clearly express the point I want to make?
- Are my sentences well written?

Read the revision of the article about robots on the next page. Look for the changes. Then answer each question below. The items listed in the box above may help you answer these questions.

1. Why did the writer add the first paragraph? *To add a little more introduction.*

2. Why was a sentence moved from paragraph 2 to paragraph 3? *The sentence fit better in paragraph 3*

3. Why was a sentence taken out of paragraph 2? *Because that paragraph is about C-3po and R-2D2*

4. Why was a sentence added to paragraph 3? *It explained more about Todays robots*

The following example shows the kinds of revisions that are needed for the article about robots. See if you can figure out why each change was made.

Revising

The robots we see in movies often make us think that robots are science fiction and there are no robots in real life. That is not true. There are robots today, but they are not exactly like the robots we see in movies.

Robots in movies look and act more like humans then machines. ~~Real robots look more like machines then humans.~~ R2-D2 and c-3PO, the robots in the Star Wars movies, have lots of human characteristics. They ~~feel~~ are loyal, and ^they form friendships. They do things like translate langauges and deliver secret plans. ~~R2-D2 can only beep and whistle.~~ C-3PO even has creativity circuits that enable him to make up stories.

Real robots look more like machines than humans.
~~The real robots we have today are more like smart machines.~~ They have artificial intelligence and ^they can do jobs in factories. They ^robots do dangerous work **There are also robots that** like handling toxic materials and defusing bombs. ^do household chores. You can buy a robot vacuum cleaner. It's a flat oval machine that moves over the floor. It senses where dirt is and goes there to suck it up. When its done, it goes back to it's base.

The robots in ^science fiction ~~sci-fi~~ movies and real robots have some things in common They do work that is normally done by humans and ^they can replace humans in certain kinds of jobs.

Lesson 1 — The Writing Process

4 Proofreading

When you have revised your work and are happy with it, the last thing you do is **proofread**. That means you read what you have written again and check to be sure everything is right. You look for mistakes in grammar and usage. You also look for mistakes in spelling, capitalization, and punctuation. You proofread to make sure that

- subjects and verbs agree
- pronoun forms are right
- punctuation marks are used correctly
- all words are spelled correctly
- names are capitalized
- titles are underlined or in quotes

When you proofread, you can use some of these marks to show your changes.

	Proofreading Symbols	
∧	Add letters or words.	List ideas ∧about your topic.
⊙	Add a period.	That is not true⊙
≡	Capitalize a letter.	R2-D2 and c̲-3PO are loyal.
⌒	Close up space.	They form friend⌒ships.
⌄	Add a comma.	There are robots today⌄but they are different.
/	Make a capital letter lowercase.	The /Robots today are different.
¶	Begin a new paragraph.	¶ Real robots look like machines.
✐	Delete letters or words.	Real robots look like r✐eal machines.
∩	Switch the position of letters or words.	The robots are today like machines.

Practice using proofreading marks with this paragraph.

Real robots usual⌄ look more machines, than humans. they have artificial intelligence can do jobs in Factories They do dangerous work handling like toxic materials and defusing bombs.

Now look at the corrections that need to be made when you proofread the article about robots. Circle the proofreading corrections in the draft below. You should find eight corrections.

Proofreading

The robots we see in movies often make us think that robots are science fiction and that there are no robots in real life. That is not true. There are robots today, but they are not exactly like the robots we see in movies.

Robots in movies look and act more like humans ~~then~~ **than** machines. ~~Real robots look more like machines then humans.~~ R2-D2 and C-3PO, the robots in the Star Wars movies, have lots of human characteristics. They ~~feel~~ **are** loyal, and **they** form friendships. They do things like translate ~~langauges~~ **languages** and deliver secret plans. ~~R2-D2 can only beep and whistle.~~ C-3PO even has creativity circuits that enable him to make up stories.

Real robots look more like machines than humans. ~~The real robots we have today are more like smart machines.~~ They have artificial intelligence and **they** can do jobs in factories. **Robots** do dangerous work like handling toxic materials and defusing bombs. **There are also robots that do household chores.** You can buy a robot vacuum cleaner. It's a flat oval machine that moves over the floor. It senses where dirt is and goes there to suck it up. When ~~its~~ **it's** done, it goes back to ~~it's~~ **its** base.

The robots in ~~sci-fi~~ **science fiction** movies and real robots have some things in common. They do work that is normally done by humans and **they** can replace humans in certain kinds of jobs.

Your Turn to Read the Question

Read the test question carefully. To understand what is being asked, look for key words and underline them.

> Which is a better way to communicate with your friends, on the phone or by e-mail? Write an essay that compares and contrasts the two ways to communicate.
>
> When writing your essay, be sure to do the following:
> - follow all the steps of the writing process
> - tell how the two ways are alike
> - tell how the two ways are different

Your Turn to Plan

Plan
Write
Edit
Check

Use this space to plan your writing. You can use this compare and contrast chart or a Venn diagram to organize your ideas.

What's Different?

Subject: phone	Subject: e-mail
takes less time	you can send pictures
Answer it either	costs less to send far.
express emotion more	more time to plan to say
	send it any time because they don't have to answer right away

What's the Same?

used to communicate

talk long distance

Finish Line Writing 11

Your Turn to Write a Draft

Now that you have thought about the topic and have organized your ideas, write a draft of your essay. Your draft should explain how the two ways to communicate are alike and how they are different.

There are many ways to communicate today. The phone, an older invention, is used worldwide. E-mail the newer way to talk is for some much more convenient.

E-mail often e-mail is better for long distance for two reasons you can send it any time of day or night because they don't have to answer it right away They can leave it to the next day, and no matter how far you send it you won't spend any money.

When you have written your draft, reread it carefully. Then revise the content and structure if they need to be changed. Finally, proofread your revision for spelling, punctuation, capitalization, and grammar. Then write your final answer on your own paper.

Lesson 1 — The Writing Process

© The Continental Press, Inc. Do not duplicate.

Your Turn to Score Writing

Use this rubric to review your own writing. Then exchange your paper with another student. Review each other's writing, and give it a score based on this rubric. Discuss ways you can each improve your writing.

Rubric for Writing Comparison and Contrast

Score 3
- The writing answers all parts of the test question.
- There are at least two clear comparisons and two clear contrasts.
- Transitional words and phrases connect the ideas.
- Each paragraph has a topic sentence that clearly states the subject.
- Supporting details are organized in a logical order.
- The writing is easy to read and stays on the subject.
- There are almost no mistakes in grammar, capitalization, punctuation, and spelling.

Score 2
- The writing answers almost all parts of the test question.
- There are two generally clear comparisons and two contrasts.
- Transitional words and phrases connect most ideas.
- A topic sentence stating the subject is missing or unclear.
- Some supporting details are missing or are not in a logical order.
- The writing is fairly easy to read and mostly stays on the subject.
- There are some mistakes in grammar, capitalization, punctuation, and spelling.

Score 1
- The writing answers only part of the test question.
- There are fewer than two comparisons or two contrasts.
- Very few transitional words and phrases are used to connect ideas.
- More than one topic sentence is missing or unclear.
- Many supporting details are missing and are not in a logical order.
- The writing is not easy to read or is off the subject in many places.
- There are several mistakes in grammar, capitalization, punctuation, and spelling.

© The Continental Press, Inc. Do not duplicate.

Lesson 2: Writing a Paragraph

Most of the things you read or write are made up of several paragraphs. Each paragraph focuses on one topic or main idea.

The Topic Sentence

The **topic sentence** should tell what the central or main idea of the paragraph is. The rest of the sentences will provide details or information about the main idea. Look for the main idea and the topic sentence in this paragraph. Underline the topic sentence.

> Some people wonder why there are still trains in this age of aviation. Trains are an important part of the transportation network across America and around the world. They move both people and things from place to place. Often trains carry freight to major trade centers. The freight cars are then moved to trucks that take them to specific destinations. People can also make both short and longer journeys by train. Train travel is slower, of course, than flying, but there are other benefits. Trains are often more comfortable, and train travel is less expensive. Trains are going to be with us for a long time.

In the paragraph above, which sentence gives you a general idea of what the whole paragraph is about?

- In the paragraph the second sentence is the topic sentence.
- The topic is "trains."
- The topic sentence tells you that you are going to read about why trains are still important.

For each group of sentences below, circle the letter of the one that is most likely to be the topic sentence of a paragraph. Remember that the topic sentence tells the central or main idea.

1. a. Some kites are shaped like diamonds, while some have triangular shapes.
   b. Flying kites is a very popular hobby among kids as well as adults.
   c. The tail of a kite can be short or long.
   d. You can make a kite from a kit or from materials you have around the house.

2. a. To score in football, you need to reach the end zone with the ball.
   b. The football field is divided into ten-yard segments.
   c. Football is one of the most popular sports in the United States.
   d. The Super Bowl is football's final championship game in the United States.

3. a. Vegetables are usually full of essential vitamins.
   b. A serving of vegetables is usually a half cup, raw or cooked.
   c. Vegetables are usually low in calories.
   d. Studies on nutrition have shown that we need three to five servings of vegetables per day.

4. a. Over 70 percent of American households with children have a computer.
   b. Children use computers to stay in touch with friends, play games, and do homework.
   c. Some children spend too much time in front of the computer.
   d. Sales of video game consoles to families with children are not rising due to the popularity of computer video games.

5. a. People sleep in 90-minute cycles that repeat many times each night.
   b. When you sleep, your brain and body recharge so that you have energy to work well again the next day.
   c. Children need the most sleep in order to help their bodies grow.
   d. Sleep is a critical part of staying healthy.

Writing a Topic Sentence

Write a topic sentence for each of the following paragraphs. To start, look at the topic and read the rest of the paragraph. Ask yourself what the central idea about the topic is. Then write a topic sentence. Notice that the topic sentence does not always have to be the first sentence in a paragraph.

TIP
Remember to indent the first line of a paragraph when you are writing.

Topic: Video Games

　　Have you ever played video games? _____ _____ They can be played on a game system connected to a television, or they can be played on a computer. Video games have been shown to help students learn strategy and think logically. Professions from medicine to the military use video games to train people. Video games help them learn techniques they have to use in real life.

Topic: Streetcars in Cities

_____

The old streetcars' wheels ride on rails embedded in the street. Usually, lines overhead supply electric power to the streetcar. Power can also come from a "third rail" next to the rails the car rides on. In the city of San Francisco, streetcars are called cable cars because an electric cable pulls the cars up and down the city's big hills.

Lesson 2 — Writing a Paragraph

Filling in the Details

A good paragraph makes sense. Every sentence should be about the topic, and the sentences should be in some order. Here is a flow chart that shows how the paragraph about trains on page 14 is organized by details.

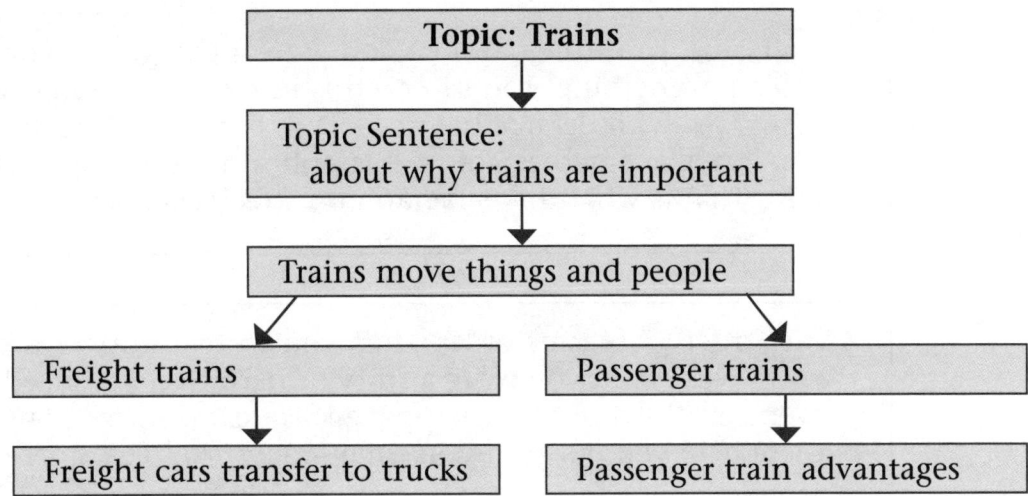

Ending a Paragraph

If you are writing just one paragraph, you should end with a **closing sentence**, or conclusion. "Trains are going to be with us for a long time" is the closing sentence in the paragraph about trains. It finishes the paragraph and makes a conclusion about the topic.

Use the following sentences to write a paragraph. First, decide which sentence is the topic sentence. Next, number the sentences in order. Then, using your order, write the sentences in the form of a paragraph on the lines below. Finally, write a concluding sentence.

> Older streetcars and trolleys ran right down the middle of the street.
> Light rail transit systems are today's version of the streetcar.
> Light rail systems in cities usually run on the side of the road.
> There are light rail systems in cities, between towns, and from cities to suburbs.
> Like streetcars, light rails run on electricity, and they do not pollute the air.

_____

_____

_____

_____

Finish Line Writing

Organizing a Paragraph

There is more than one way to organize a paragraph. The order you choose will depend on the kind of writing you are doing. Here are some ways to organize information in a paragraph.

Details and Examples When you write a paragraph, you often want to explain something. You can do this in two ways. You can follow your main idea with details that support it, as the paragraph on trains does. You can also organize your paragraph so that examples support the main idea. That is what the paragraph on streetcars does.

Time Order Use time order when you write a story or a personal narrative. When you write a story or narrative, you need to tell the events in the order they happened. Transition words and phrases such as these help you put things in time order: *first, then, after that, later, finally*.

Spatial Order Use spatial order when you are describing a scene or view. Spatial order means that you are explaining the location of things in your description. If you want to describe a new park, you might use transition words and phrases such as *close by, in the distance,* or *around*.

Writing for a Test

Plan
Write
Edit
Check

Sometimes you must write an answer to a question on a test. These questions may be called "brief" or "short" response. Your answer should be a paragraph. Test-taking time is limited, but you can follow these steps to write your answer.

1. Underline the key words to be sure you understand the question.
2. Think about what you want to say.
3. Decide which organizational plan you will use.
4. Write your topic sentence first, then finish your paragraph.
5. Check your answer. You can still make changes.

Answering a Test Question

Read this article about computers and the test question that follows it.

Computers Are Everywhere

The age of technology has reached into the everyday lives of American families. Over 70 percent of families with children now have computers. Computers are used for everything from playing games to shopping to paying bills. Many children do their homework on computers, and they surf the Internet for fun as well as for information for schoolwork.

People who do not have a computer at home still use them in many places. Most schools have computers available for their students to use. Many local libraries have computers for their customers to use as well as for information about the books on their shelves.

Many jobs require people to use computers. Of course, offices use computers. Salespeople and deliverers use computers to keep track of their work. If you decide to apply for a job at the supermarket, you may use a computer to fill out your application. And, if you get the job, you will use a computer when you work. Learning to use a computer is a basic skill for everyone these days.

Do you use a computer for schoolwork, for playing games, or for communicating with friends? Write a paragraph about an experience you have had using a computer.

Here is how Aimée wrote her answer to the test question. First she underlined important parts of the question and made some notes. She knew she would need to write a narrative, or a story, about her own experience with computers. She decided to use time order to organize the events in her story.

To plan her writing, Aimée wrote down the events that she wanted to tell. Then she arranged them in the order in which they occurred.

1. Rachel e-mailed me last Saturday
2. She wanted to play a computer game
3. I learned how to play the week before
4. We began to play
5. She taught me tricks
6. I improved and beat her
7. I stopped playing to have dinner
8. After dinner I called her to thank her
9. We decided to play the next day

With her plan completed, Aimée used the events that she listed to write her short response in the form of a paragraph. Read Aimée's paragraph below. Then find and circle the words that show time order. Underline Aimée's topic sentence and her concluding sentence.

    Last Saturday afternoon my cousin Rachel, who lives in Utah, e-mailed me. She wanted me to play a computer game with her. She had been practicing the game for three months. I had just learned how to play the week before. We both logged on and began to play. While we were playing she showed me a lot of new tricks. By the end of the afternoon, I had improved so much that I actually beat Rachel in one game. My mom finally made us stop playing so I could have dinner. After dinner I called Rachel to thank her for helping me improve. We made plans to play again the next day.

Lesson 2 — Writing a Paragraph

Your Turn to Read the Question

The reading passage on page 19 ends with this sentence: "Learning to use a computer is a basic skill for everyone these days." Explain what the writer means by this statement. Be sure to include a topic sentence that states your main idea. Support your topic sentence with your own examples or by using details or information from the passage.

Read the test question carefully. Then underline the key words in order to understand what the question is asking you to do.

 Remember: when you are taking a writing test, your time is limited. Be sure to divide up your time to allow for each step: Plan, Write, Edit, and Check.

Plan Write Edit Check

Your Turn to Plan
Using your own paper, plan your short response.

Your Turn to Write
On the lines below, write a draft of your paragraph, using the notes you made while planning. Review your draft. Is the main idea clear? Do the other sentences support the main idea? Does the order of your paragraph make sense? Did you write a concluding sentence?

_____
_____
_____
_____
_____
_____
_____

Your Turn to Edit and Check
Proofread your draft. Then write your final version of the paragraph on a separate sheet of paper.

Finish Line Writing

Lesson 3 Writing Sentences

Sentences are the building blocks of writing. A sentence is a group of words that expresses a complete thought.

Subject and Predicate

Every sentence has two parts: a complete subject and a complete predicate.

┌—complete subject—┐ ┌————complete predicate————┐
Our federal government conducts a census every ten years.

The **subject** tells the person, place, thing, or idea a sentence is about. It also tells who or what is doing the action in a sentence.	The **predicate** tells something about the subject. It identifies what the subject does, is, has, or feels.

A **complete subject** can be one word or several words. The key word in the complete subject is the simple subject. It identifies what the subject is about. The simple subject is often a **noun**, although sometimes the subject is a pronoun. The following pronouns can be used as subjects:

Subject Pronouns	
Singular	Plural
I	we
you	you
he, she, it	they

<u>She</u> filled out the census.

<u>It</u> was easy to fill out.

Do <u>you</u> have a stamp?

<u>We</u> will mail the census today.

A **complete predicate**, like a complete subject, can be one word or several words. The key word in the complete predicate is the simple predicate, or **verb**. The verb may be a single word, or it may have a helping verb.

Birds <u>sing</u>.   The birds <u>are singing</u>.

Verbs such as *sing* are called **action verbs**. Action verbs are sometimes followed by an object. An object, like a subject, is often a noun and can be one word or several words. The object receives the action of the verb. Look at the object nouns underlined in these sentences.

I play the <u>piano</u>.   We sing <u>"The Star Spangled Banner"</u> during assembly.

An object can also be a pronoun. Look at the object pronouns underlined in these sentences.

Object Pronouns	
Singular	Plural
me	us
you	you
him, her, it	them

We sing <u>it</u> every day.

Jared heard <u>them</u> from outside.

Anna sent <u>you</u> the music.

Sara told <u>me</u> about the play.

Verbs such as *is, were,* and *seem* are called **linking verbs.** The verb "links" the subject and the noun after the verb. Here each linking verb is in bold type, and the noun it connects to the subject is underlined.

Those books **are** <u>novels</u>.   Lara **is** a <u>heroine</u> in that novel.

A. Circle each complete subject and underline each complete predicate.

1. Green plants play a key role in the cycle of nature.
2. Our early ancestors gathered plants from the wild to eat.
3. Certain plants form the basis of different diets around the world.
4. These essential plants are called staple foods.
5. Many useful fibers are found in the stems, leaves, and seeds of plants.

B. Circle each simple subject and underline each simple predicate.

1. The Civil War was a conflict between the North and the South.
2. It lasted from 1861 to 1865.
3. The North had more resources than the South.
4. Soldiers on both sides marched into battle to the fife and drum.
5. Women volunteered as nurses and hospital workers.

C. Underline each action verb and its object. If the verb has a helping verb, circle it.

1. The founding fathers of the United States adopted a system of government similar to that of the ancient Greeks.
2. They wanted a democracy.
3. Our federal government has three branches.
4. Each branch can check the decisions of the other branches.
5. This arrangement is called the system of checks and balances.

Fragments

Remember a sentence needs both a subject and a predicate to express a complete thought. If one or both of these parts is missing, the sentence is incomplete. An incomplete sentence is called a **sentence fragment.**

Although a fragment may begin with a capital letter and end with a punctuation mark, it is not a sentence. A fragment may lack a subject, a predicate, or both.

Correcting Sentence Fragments

Here each fragment is corrected by adding its missing sentence part. To help you identify which part is missing, each subject is underlined once, and each predicate is underlined twice.

This sentence fragment is missing a **predicate.**

Fragment   The dog in the house.

Complete   The dog in the house **barked.**
Sentence

This sentence fragment is missing a **subject.**

Fragment   Is playing the piano.

Complete   **My brother** is playing the piano.
Sentence

This sentence fragment is missing **both a subject and a predicate.**

Fragment   After the concert.

Complete   **Everyone went to Tom's house** after the concert.
Sentence

Another way to correct a sentence fragment is to attach the fragment to the sentence that comes before or after it.

Here the fragment *After the concert* is corrected by combining it with a complete sentence that comes before it.

Fragment   The concert was great. Everyone went to Tom's house. *After the concert.* He had a lot of food for all of us.

Corrected   The concert was great. Everyone went to Tom's house **after the concert**. He had a lot of food for all of us.

A. Cross out each group of words that is a fragment. Then circle the simple subject and underline the simple predicate in each group of words that is a sentence.

1. The *Titanic* hit an iceberg.
2. The ice tore a hole in the ship.
3. Sent an SOS.
4. People rushed to the lifeboats.
5. Men, women, and children.
6. Not enough lifeboats.
7. The mighty ship sank.
8. Over 1,500 passengers.

B. Write an *F* on the line before each group of words that is a fragment. Write an *S* before each complete sentence.

_____ 1. Aardvarks are similar to anteaters.
_____ 2. In many ways.
_____ 3. Aardvarks live in Africa.
_____ 4. Feed mostly on ants and termites.
_____ 5. Aardvarks about four to six feet long.
_____ 6. A long tail and a long snout.
_____ 7. Aardvarks can dig a deep tunnel.
_____ 8. Within a few minutes.
_____ 9. Their very sharp claws.
_____ 10. Can easily tear open insects' nests.

C. On the lines below, correct each fragment you identified in exercise B by combining it with another sentence or adding a subject or verb.

_____
_____
_____
_____
_____
_____

Finish Line Writing 25

Run-on Sentences

A **run-on sentence** is two or more sentences that run together with commas or without any punctuation. This creates confusion because a reader does not know where one thought ends and the next thought begins.

Run-on Sentences We will have to hurry now, we will be late. (comma)
We will have to hurry now we will be late. (no punctuation)

There are two ways to correct a run-on sentence. One way is to write each complete thought as a separate sentence.

Two Separate Sentences We will have to hurry now. We will be late.

Another way is to use a conjunction to combine each complete thought to create a **compound sentence**. A compound sentence is made up of two simple sentences that are joined by a comma and a conjunction such as *and, or, but,* or *so.*

Compound Sentences We will have to hurry now, **or** we will be late.

A. First, correct each run-on sentence below by writing it as two complete sentences. Then, correct it by writing it as a compound sentence.

1. Kirsten likes to sing she also loves to dance.

   _____
   _____

2. The Carey family cooked the turkey we brought the pies.

   _____
   _____

3. I will see a movie on Saturday, I will clean my room on Sunday.

   _____
   _____

4. The old car needed a lot of repairs we decided to buy a new one.

   _____
   _____

Lesson 3 — Writing Sentences

Capitalization

Always capitalize the first word of a sentence.

Incorrect   most of those bananas are too ripe.

Correct   Most of those bananas are too ripe.

Capitalize the names of people, places, and holidays.

People	Places	Holidays
James Murphy	Grand Canyon	Memorial Day
Shana Ferrara	Paris, France	Labor Day
Ian Goldsmith	Tremont Street	Hanukkah

A. Circle the word or words in each sentence that need a capital letter.

1. it's so hard to get everyone in the family to pose for a picture.
2. on thanksgiving, we had 14 relatives for dinner.
3. they wanted to have a picture to use for a christmas card.
4. uncle roger said he would set up the camera.
5. he told us to pretend we were in hawaii.
6. my cousin amal wanted to pretend we were in the sahara desert in africa.
7. aunt sarah wanted to pretend we were on the top of the statue of liberty.
8. dad wanted us to pretend we just won a new car.
9. mom didn't care what we pretended.
10. she just wanted us to smile.

Punctuation

A sentence begins with a capital letter and ends with a punctuation mark.

Periods

A sentence that makes a statement or a command ends with a period.

Statement   The children learned a lot at the museum.

Command   Don't forget to be on time for the soccer playoffs.

Question Marks

A sentence that asks a question ends with a question mark.

Question   Have you seen our new cocker spaniel puppy?

Exclamation Marks

A sentence that expresses a strong feeling ends with an exclamation mark.

Exclamation   That drawing you made for the art show is fantastic!

A. Add the correct end punctuation to each sentence below.

1. Did you know that honeybees live in hives
2. The worker bee is the smallest honeybee in the colony
3. There is only one queen in a hive
4. The queen can lay up to 2,000 eggs per day
5. There is a beehive in the tree Watch out

Commas

A compound sentence is two complete sentences joined by a comma and a conjunction such as *and, or, but,* or *so*.

Compound Sentence   I love the snow, **but** I don't like the cold weather.

B. Write the correct punctuation and conjunction (*and, or, but, so*) for each of the following compound sentences.

1. Some people say 45 degrees Fahrenheit is cold _____ others say 0 degrees Fahrenheit is cold.

2. Snow can make roads slippery _____ drivers need to slow down in a snowstorm.

3. Winter in northern states can be six months long _____ it can be very windy and cold.

4. It is possible to walk on thick ice _____ even thick ice can have weak spots.

5. Wear a warm hat when you are outside _____ your ears might get frostbitten.

Lesson 3 — Writing Sentences

Your Turn to Revise and Edit

A. Revise the following paragraph by correcting all fragments and run-on sentences. Cross out each mistake and write the correction above it.

   Trains are an important part. Of the transportation network. Across America and around the world. They move both people and things from place to place. Carry freight to major centers. The freight is then moved to trucks. Take it to specific destinations.

   Some people prefer traveling in trains. Train travel is slower than flying most riders don't mind because trains are more comfortable train travel is cheaper.

B. Edit the following paragraph to correct all mistakes in capitalization and punctuation. Cross out each mistake and write the correction above it.

   Early forms of transportation included wagon trains, Thousands of people traveled across the plains and over the mountains in canvas covered wagons. most of the passengers were heading west because of the california Gold Rush. Everyone wanted to get rich quickly? Many did not make it and the trails became littered with broken wagons dead animals and human skeletons. Do you think you would have enjoyed traveling by wagon train.

Lesson 4 Main Idea and Details

Look out the window of the room you are in. There is a good chance you will see a tree. Someone planted the tree, and it may have been on Arbor Day. Read the following article to learn how Arbor Day began.

The Story of Arbor Day

In 1854, J. Sterling Morton and his wife settled in the Nebraska Territory. Not long after moving into their new home, they noticed that something was missing. There were no trees. The Nebraska landscape was mostly treeless plains. The Mortons knew that trees would prevent soil erosion and provide shade. They soon planted trees around their own property. Morton began to write newspaper articles to encourage other people to plant trees, too.

When Morton became secretary of the Nebraska Territory, he decided to do something about the lack of trees. He proposed a tree-planting holiday, and he called it Arbor Day. On the first Arbor Day in Nebraska over one million trees were planted. In 1885, Nebraska made Arbor Day a legal holiday and set the date for April 22, Morton's birthday. Other states soon followed with their own Arbor Days. Before long, the tradition of planting trees on Arbor Day had taken hold across the country.

Today most states observe Arbor Day on the last Friday in April, which is also national Arbor Day. Some states have Arbor Day at a different time when the weather is better for planting trees. No matter what day it is celebrated, tree planting on Arbor Day has become a beloved tradition. It is celebrated in many countries around the world.

Reading the Question

In this part of the lesson, you will see how one student, Dalia, used facts and information from the article to write an answer to a test question.

Dalia knew it was important to read the test question more than once. She underlined the important words and made some notes.

> A grove of shade trees near your neighborhood is going to be made into a park with benches and picnic tables. It will be named Morton Park after J. Sterling Morton. Write an <u>article</u> for your neighborhood <u>newsletter</u> explaining who J. Sterling Morton was and why the name is appropriate for the park. In your article be sure to include
> - a <u>main idea</u> about why the name is appropriate
> - <u>facts and details</u> from the article that support the main idea

Dalia underlined the words *article, newsletter, main idea* and *facts and details*, and she made these notes:

topic - J. Sterling Morton

audience - neighbors

Morton started Arbor Day

A million trees were planted the first time

Other states started Arbor Day

It's a national day now

It's even in other countries

people plant trees every year

Dalia spent about three minutes reading the question and looking back at the article.

Finish Line Writing

Planning to Write

Once you understand the test question, you can plan your writing using a graphic organizer. Dalia decided to use a web. She wrote her main idea in the center.

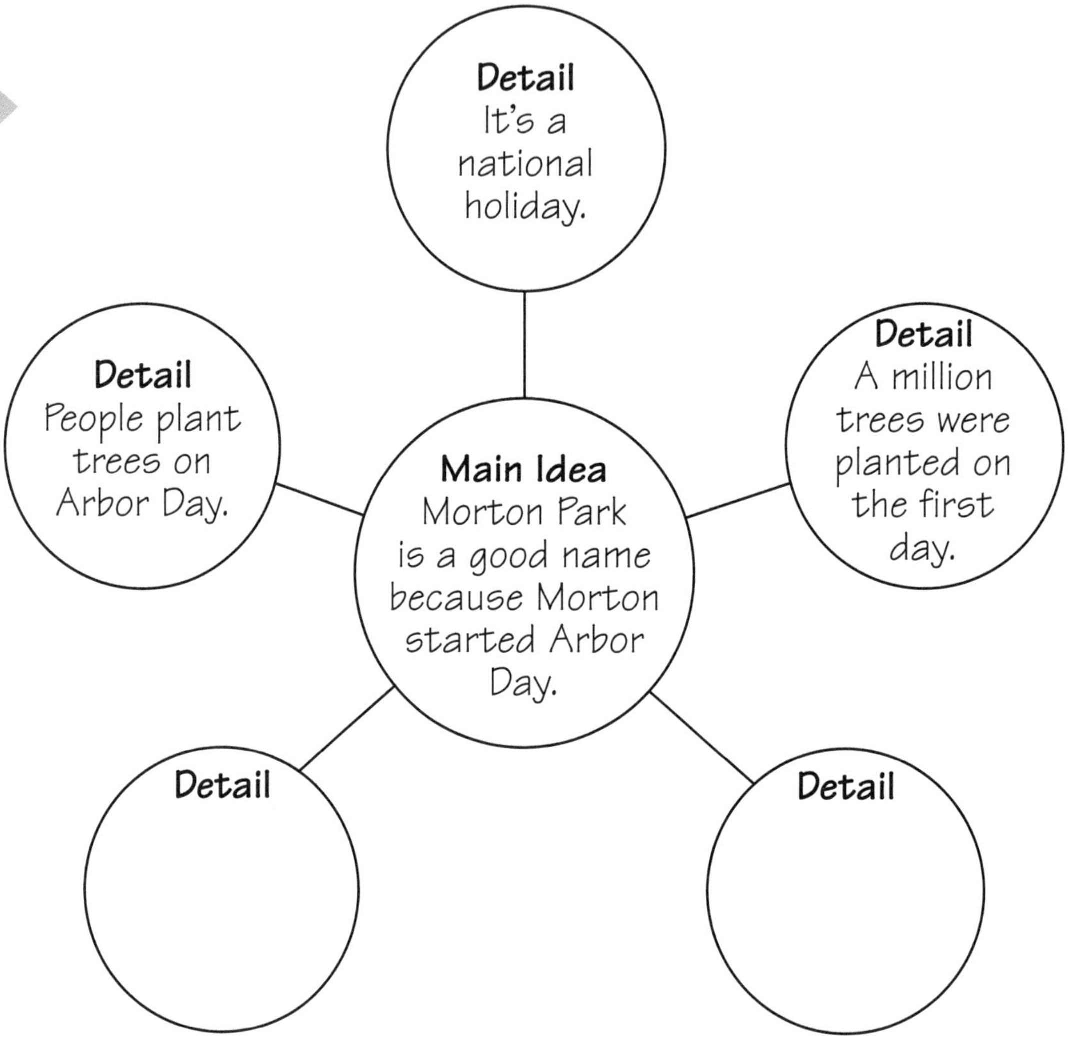

Prewriting

- **Main Idea**: Morton Park is a good name because Morton started Arbor Day.
  - **Detail**: It's a national holiday.
  - **Detail**: A million trees were planted on the first day.
  - **Detail**: People plant trees on Arbor Day.
  - **Detail**:
  - **Detail**:

Completing the Plan

Which items below also fit in the chart as details supporting Dalia's main idea? Check the items that fit.

1. ___ Morton and his wife loved trees.
2. ___ Some states have Arbor Day at different times because of the weather.
3. ___ Nebraska used to be nothing but treeless plains.
4. ___ Morton knew that trees provide shade.

Writing a Draft

Here is how Dalia developed her draft.

Drafting

Morton Park is the perfect name for our new neighborhood park. It's the one with the lovely grove of shade trees. The name "Morton" means J Sterling Morton. This is the person who started Arbor day, which is a special holiday for planting trees.

Morton started Arbor Day because his wife and he loved trees. When he moved to Nebraska, they found there were no trees where they lived. There was just a plain He knew that trees were needed because they provided shade. They liked seeing the flowering trees too. When he became Secretary of the Nebraska Territory he had Day declared a holiday. He hoped that some would plant trees on that day. On that first Arbor Day in 1872, over a million trees were planted. Arbor Day is still celebrated today. Arbor Day is now a national holiday. People from all over the world also celebrate this day. And plant trees. We should name our park after Sterling J. Morton because of his love of trees. It is a good way to honor J. Sterling Morton, and we should name our park after him. Thanks to him, the world today has more trees.

1. Write Dalia's topic sentence here. _____

2. What is the most important detail that Dalia has included? _____

Revising and Proofreading

Here is Dalia's revised draft. Read it carefully and answer the questions below.

Revising

Morton Park is the perfect name for our new neighborhood park. ~~It's the one~~ with the lovely grove of shade trees. The name "Morton" ~~means~~ honors J Sterling Morton. ~~This~~ He is the person who started Arbor day, which is a special holiday for planting trees.

Morton started Arbor Day because his wife and he loved trees. When ~~he~~ they moved to Nebraska, they found there were no trees where they lived. There was just a plain He knew that trees were needed because they provided shade. ~~They liked seeing the flowering trees too.~~ When he became Secretary of the Nebraska Territory he had Day declared a holiday. He hoped that ~~some~~ people would plant trees on that day. On that first Arbor Day in 1872, over a million trees were planted.

¶ Arbor Day is still celebrated today, and ~~Arbor Day~~ is now a national holiday. People ~~from~~ all over the world also celebrate this day by planting ~~And plant~~ trees. We should name our park after Sterling J. Morton because of his love of trees. ~~It is a good way to honor J. Sterling Morton, and we should name our park after him.~~ Thanks to him, the world today has more trees.

1. Why did Dalia cross out two sentences? _____

_____

2. Which sentences did she combine? _____

_____

Proofreading

Proofread Dalia's draft for five more mistakes. Write your corrections above.

Your Turn to Read

Read the following article on how to plant a tree. Then answer the test question.

Directions for Planting a Tree

Are you planning to plant a tree this Arbor Day? Before you begin, you will want to learn the basics of tree planting. With planning and care, the tree you plant will survive and grow, giving you pleasure for years to come.

Before you begin, find out if this is the right time of year to plant a tree. Climate plays a big role in deciding when to plant. Newly planted trees do best with moderate temperatures and rainfall. Trees need time to develop roots and get used to the temperature before the heat of summer or the cold of winter begins. That's why spring and fall are usually the best time to plant a tree. In the southern United States, the warm winter means you can plant a tree any time of the year.

1. Choose a tree that is right for your climate. Don't try to force a warm weather tree to grow in cold northern areas. Check with your local tree nursery for suggestions.

2. After you have chosen your tree, you're ready to dig the hole. It should not be too deep or too narrow. The roots of the tree need room to spread out, and they need to be close enough to the surface to get oxygen. As a rule of thumb, never plant a tree deeper than the soil in which is was originally grown. The hole should be about three times the width of the tree's root structure.

3. If your tree has a root ball wrapped in burlap, lift the tree by the root ball, never by the trunk. Remove the burlap and all string and twine from the root ball.

4. Loosen the root structure with your hands. That will allow the roots to expand. Lower the tree into the hole.

5. Mix fertilizer with good soil, following the directions on the container. Fill the hole, but do not compress the soil. If you do, water will not get to the roots.

6. When the tree is planted, fertilize the soil around the planting hole to promote growth.

7. Water the base of the tree well.

Finish Line Writing

Your Turn to Read the Question

Your next step is to read the test question carefully. Underline important parts of the test question. Then answer the questions that follow.

> You have decided to give a tree to your friend in Georgia whose birthday is on Arbor Day. Write a note to your friend with suggestions for planting the tree. In your note, be sure to include
> - a main idea
> - important details and information for planting a tree

1. What kind of writing are you being asked to do?

_____

_____

2. What will the structure of your writing look like when you are done?

_____

3. Who is your audience?

_____

Your Turn to Plan

Read the question again to see where to start your planning process. To give your friend clear instructions, you need to understand the main idea of the directions and the important details.

The question tells you to provide steps for planting a tree. This means you need to isolate the key idea in each step in order to write clear directions for your friend. Use the graphic organizer below to plan your note.

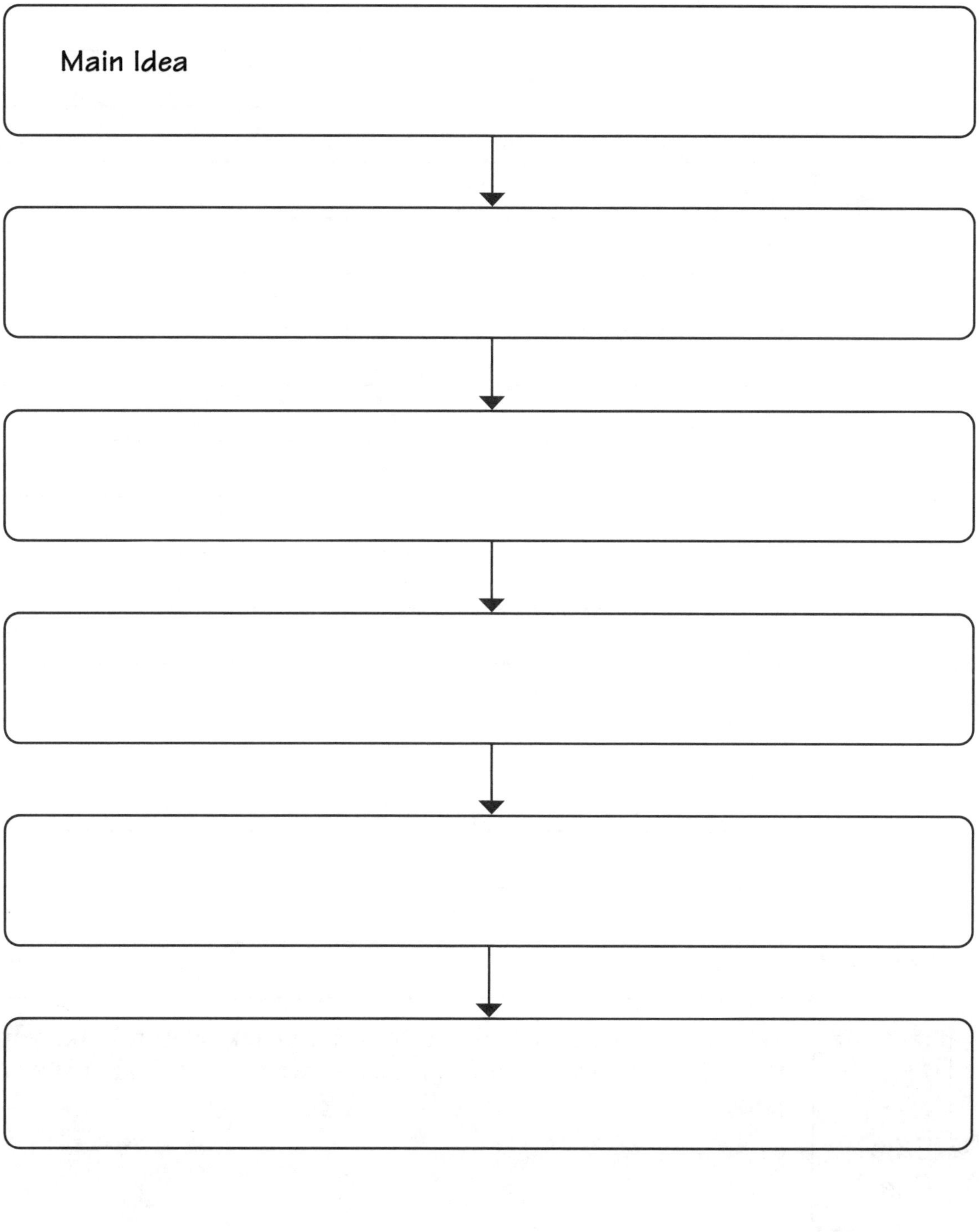

Main Idea

Finish Line Writing

Your Turn to Write a Draft

Before you write your draft, review your graphic organizer. Think about what your topic sentence should be. Are all your ideas in the correct order? Do you need to add details to make the process clearer? Remember to clearly state the main idea and use supporting details to let the reader know why you have included the information in each step.

When you have finished your draft, go back over it. Make your revisions on this page. Proofread your draft. Then write your final answer on your own paper.

Your Turn to Score Writing

Use this rubric to review your own writing. Then exchange your paper with another student. Review each other's writing, and give it a score based on this rubric. Discuss ways you can each improve your writing.

Rubric for Writing Main Idea and Details

Score 3
- The writing answers all parts of the test question.
- Each paragraph has a topic sentence that clearly states the main idea.
- The writing includes important details that clearly support the main idea.
- The writing is easy to read and stays on the subject.
- Words are used correctly and well.
- There are almost no mistakes in grammar, capitalization, punctuation, and spelling.

Score 2
- The writing answers almost all parts of the test question.
- A topic sentence stating the main idea is missing or unclear.
- The writing includes some details that support the main idea.
- The writing is fairly easy to read and mostly stays on the subject.
- Some words are misused.
- There are some mistakes in grammar, capitalization, punctuation, and spelling.

Score 1
- The writing answers only part of the test question.
- More than one topic sentence is missing or unclear.
- Many details are missing or they do not support the main idea.
- The writing is not easy to read or is off the subject in many places.
- Many words are overused or misused.
- There are several mistakes in grammar, capitalization, punctuation, and spelling.

Lesson 5: Cause and Effect

As you read this magazine article, think about the connections between events, or how one thing can cause another.

Tilly Smith, Age Ten, Helps Save Hundreds from the Tsunami

Why pay attention in geography class? Just ask the ten-year-old English schoolgirl, Tilly Smith. She helped save more than one hundred people from the tsunami that struck the coastal areas of the Indian Ocean on December 26, 2004. Tsunamis (soo-NAH-mes) are giant sea waves. Tilly was on vacation with her parents and younger sister in Phuket, Thailand. With its beautiful beaches and friendly people, Thailand is a popular winter vacation spot for tourists from Europe.

On the morning of the tsunami, Tilly and her family were sitting on Maikhao Beach. They watched as the tide rushed out, sucking water out to sea and away from the shore. Tilly noticed how bubbly and strange the water looked. This odd activity rang a bell. Just two weeks before, her teacher, Mr. Kearney, had explained how an earthquake under the ocean can cause a giant sea wave, or tsunami. She also learned how the sea looks and acts before a giant wave hits shore. The class even saw a video of one.

In a flash, Tilly realized that a tsunami, the subject that Mr. Kearney had been teaching, was about to happen—right here and right now. No one else on the beach seemed to realize what was happening. She screamed at her mother to tell her what she knew and that they had to get off the beach. The Smiths yelled at the other tourists to run, and everyone raced up to higher ground and their hotel. All of the people on Maikhao Beach escaped the giant waves. They were incredibly lucky. At the end of the day, the tsunami had taken more lives than any other natural disaster in recent history.

The people from Maikhao Beach have Tilly to thank for their lives. And who does Tilly thank? Mr. Kearney, her teacher.

Reading the Question

In this part of the lesson, you will see how a student, Matt, used the information from the article to write the answer to a test question.

The first thing Matt did was to read the test question carefully.

> Write an essay telling why Tilly Smith was able to help people during the tsunami. Explain what experiences caused Tilly to recognize danger.
>
> In your explanation, be sure to include
> - your main idea
> - two or more causes and their effect
> - transition words such as *because, since, so, as a result*

After Matt read the question, he made a few notes to help him remember the key points of the question.

What I will write about: how a girl saved people's lives

How I will organize: cause and effect

I must include: two or more causes and the effect

my main idea

transition words

Matt spent about three minutes reading the test question. He made sure he knew what the question was asking before he began to plan his writing. Matt knew that taking time now to understand the question would save him time when he began writing.

Finish Line Writing

Planning to Write

The next step after reading the question is recognizing **cause and effect** relationships. For the question about Tilly Smith, Matt needs to find out how two or more events caused one effect.

After Matt identified the causes and effect, he decided to use a graphic organizer to make sure that the causes occur before the effect and that the effect follows in logical order. Matt made the chart below.

CAUSE
Tilly learned about tsunamis in geography class and even saw a video.

CAUSE
Tilly saw the tide and the water that looked like the video.

EFFECT
Tilly realized that a tsunami was coming and saved the people on Maikhao Beach.

Prewriting

Completing the Plan

Matt looked over his graphic organizer. He decided to begin his answer by stating the effect first. Matt then listed his ideas and some details in the order he would write them. Use the chart and the article to complete Matt's list.

1. Tilly saved the people on Maikhao Beach from the tsunami. [effect]

2. Tilly saw the tide rush out and noticed that the water looked bubbly and strange. [cause]

3. _____

4. _____

5. All the people ran from Maikhao Beach and were saved from the tsunami. [effect]

Lesson 5 — Cause and Effect

Writing a Draft

The next step is to use your graphic organizer or paragraph plan to write your draft. Begin your paragraph with a main idea sentence. It should state the cause or effect of your topic. This is Matt's draft.

Drafting

  Tilly Smith is an English girl who saved the lives of hundreds of people in Thailand because of what she learned in school. A tsunami is a gigantic sea wave. She was sitting on Maikhao beach when she noticed something unusual. The tide rushed out from the shor and the water looked funny and strange

  Tilly is just ten years old, but she was the only one on the beach who understood what that meant. She realize what the sea was doing was a sign a tsunami was coming. Her teacher in England had just taught the students about tsunamis. What a story she would have to tell geography class!

  She knew that a tsunami was very dangerous, so she told her mother what was happening and that they had to run from the beach. Then they quickly warned the other tourists on Maikhao Beach and they all ran to safety. So, as a result of Tilly's quick thinking hundreds of people escaped the tsunami.

Tell how this test answer is organized by identifying the following:

Topic Sentence: _____

Cause 1: _____

Cause 2: _____

Effect: _____

Revising and Proofreading

Here is how Matt revised his draft. Read the revision and answer the questions.

Revising

Tilly Smith is an English girl who saved ~~the lives of~~ hundreds of people in Thailand, **from a tsunami** because of what she learned in school. A tsunami is a gigantic sea wave. She was sitting on Maikhao beach when she noticed something unusual. The tide rushed out from the shor and the water looked ~~funny~~ **bubbly** and strange.

Tilly is just ten years old, but she was the only one on the beach who understood what that meant. She realize what the sea was doing was a sign a tsunami was coming. **because** Her teacher in England had just taught her class about tsunamis. ~~What a story she would have to tell geography class.~~

She knew that a tsunami was very dangerous, so she told her mother what was happening and that they had to run from the beach. Then they quickly warned the other tourists on Maikhao Beach and they ~~ran all~~ to safety. ~~So,~~ as a result of Tilly's quick thinking hundreds of people escaped **deadly** the tsunami.

1. What did Matt take out? _____

2. What other additions or changes did he make? _____

Proofreading

Proofread Matt's paper for four more mistakes. Write the corrections above.

Lesson 5 — Cause and Effect

Your Turn to Read

Now it's your turn to practice writing an essay that shows cause and effect for a test. The first step in this process is to read about an event.

The Indian Ocean Tsunami

The Indian Ocean tsunami of December, 2004, was one of the most destructive in history. At about 7:58 A.M. local time on December 26, an earthquake occurred deep under the Indian Ocean, 150 miles off the coast of Sumatra. The huge earthquake measured at least 9.0—one of the biggest ever recorded. The earth shook for eight minutes. Giant sea waves generated by the earthquake reached nine countries.

A tsunami can travel across the ocean at speeds up to 500 miles an hour. Between 15 and 30 minutes after the earthquake, the first tsunami hit Sumatra. The last waves of the tsunami reached Somalia, in Africa, seven hours after the earthquake. In deep ocean water, a tsunami wave may only be a foot higher than the surface of the ocean. When the wave reaches shallow waters near the coasts, it slows down. Then, the top of the wave moves faster than the bottom of the wave, which causes the wave to grow in height. The first wave that hit Thailand reached 30 feet.

Tsunamis are rare in the Indian Ocean. Most people who live in the countries affected by this tsunami had never experienced one. The tsunami came as a complete surprise. About 174,000 people died in the tsunami, and still more are missing.

Immediately after the tsunami, emergency relief efforts began. Food, water, and medical help arrived and shelters were set up for the homeless. Many countries pledged money for economic relief. The cost of relief was estimated to be between four and five billion dollars for the first five years.

One of the great tragedies of the disaster was that many lives could have been saved if a tsunami early warning system had been in place in the Indian Ocean. In the Pacific Ocean, where most tsunamis form, such a system alerts people when earthquakes or other events raise the possibility of a tsunami. Leaders from the Indian Ocean countries and organizations such as the United Nations urgently began to plan for an Indian Ocean warning system after the tsunami. Until it is ready, agencies in Hawaii and Japan will transmit warning information to the region. The system should be in place by 2006 and will help avert such disasters in the future.

Your Turn to Read the Question

Now it's your turn. Begin by reading the test question carefully. Underline important parts of the question. Then plan your answer to the question.

> Write an essay to explain the causes of the damage done by the tsunami and one useful result of the disaster.
> - Include a main idea explaining the cause and effect.
> - Use details from the article to support your main idea.
> - Use transition words such as *because*, *since*, *so*, and *as a result*.

1. What kind of writing are you being asked to do?

   _____

2. Why is it important to use transition words?

   _____

3. Who is your audience?

   _____

Lesson 5 — Cause and Effect

Your Turn to Plan

Use this cause and effect chart to plan your writing.

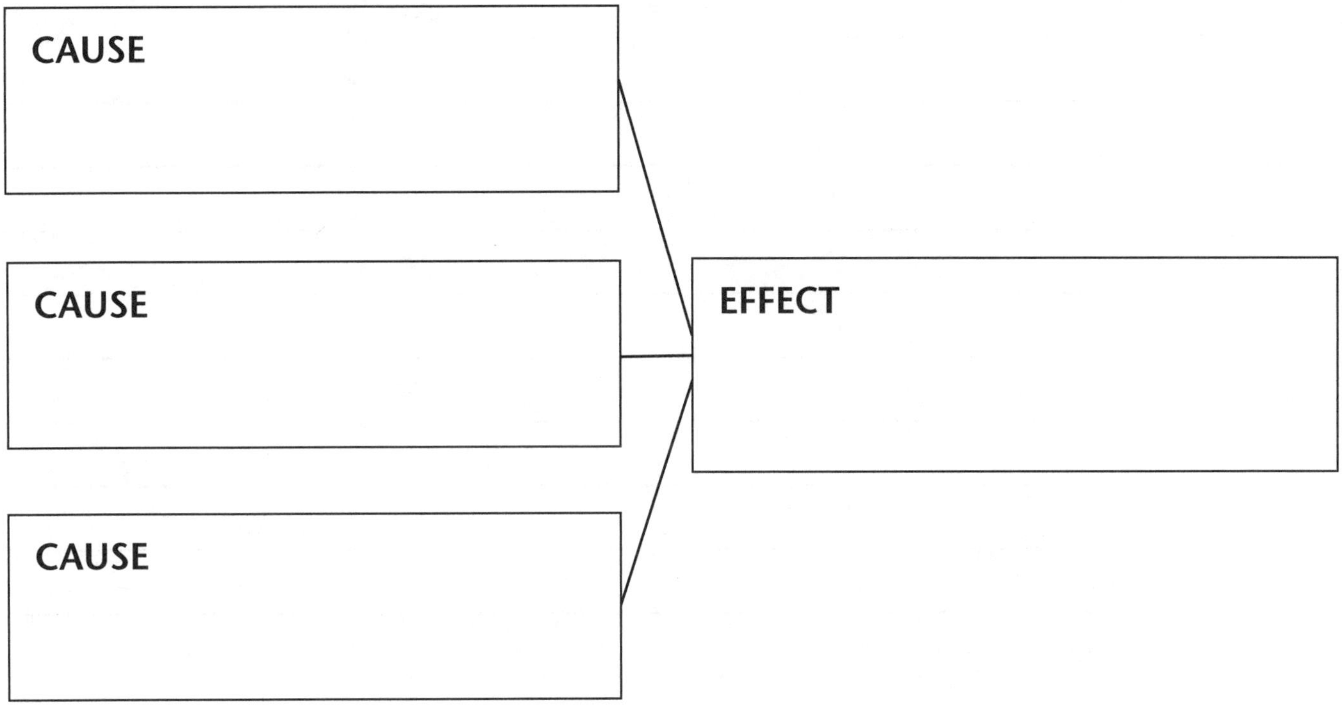

CAUSE

CAUSE

CAUSE

EFFECT

List ideas from your cause and effect chart in the order that you will present them in your writing.

1. _____

2. _____

3. _____

4. _____

5. _____

Finish Line Writing

Your Turn to Write a Draft

Use your cause and effect chart and your paragraph plan to help you as you write your draft. In the first paragraph of your essay, be sure to state the effect. Include the causes in logical order in other paragraphs. Remember to use transitional words and phrases. For example, to show cause and effect, you can use *because, since, so, cause, reason*, and *as a result*.

_____
_____
_____
_____
_____
_____
_____
_____
_____
_____
_____
_____
_____
_____
_____
_____
_____
_____
_____
_____

When you have finished your draft, go back over it. Make your revisions on this page. Proofread your draft. Then write your final answer on your own paper.

Your Turn to Score Writing

Use this rubric to review your own writing. Then exchange your paper with another student. Review each other's writing, and give it a score based on this rubric. Discuss ways you can each improve your writing.

Rubric for Writing Cause and Effect

Score 3
- The writing answers all parts of the test question.
- There are at least one clear effect and two or three causes.
- The topic sentence in the first paragraph clearly states the most important effect.
- Transition words that are specific to cause and effect connect the ideas.
- The causes are organized in a logical order.
- The writing is easy to read and stays on the subject.
- There are almost no mistakes in grammar, capitalization, punctuation, and spelling.

Score 2
- The writing answers almost all parts of the test question.
- There are at least one generally clear effect and two causes.
- The topic sentence in the first paragraph does not clearly state the most important effect.
- Transition words that are specific to cause and effect connect a few ideas.
- Most of the causes are organized in a logical order.
- The writing is fairly easy to read and mostly stays on the subject.
- There are some mistakes in grammar, capitalization, punctuation, and spelling.

Score 1
- The writing answers only part of the test question.
- The writing is unclear about what the effect and causes are.
- There is no topic sentence in the first paragraph that states the most important effect.
- There are no transition words specific to cause and effect connecting the ideas.
- The causes are not organized in a logical order.
- The writing is not easy to read or is off the subject in many places.
- There are several mistakes in grammar, capitalization, punctuation, and spelling.

Lesson 6 Comparison and Contrast

As you read this passage from a story, think about how the two characters in the story are alike and different.

from "Climbing Down"

Naomi looked at her watch. They had just one hour of daylight left. Naomi was sure that wasn't enough time to make it safely down the mountain, but Vanessa disagreed.

"We can do it, Naomi," Vanessa said in that soft, confident way of hers. Vanessa never raised her voice. She never even seemed to get tense. Even now, when the girls were lost on Saddleback Mountain, she was calm. She added, "I remember some of these landmarks. I am sure we'll find the trail just beyond those pines."

"No!" Naomi all but shouted. Her voice was full of tension, and she knew she was acting like the younger sister when, after all, she was two years older. She actually surprised herself. She had been hiking since she was five, and she had developed strong map and compass skills. Still, fear gripped her now. She knew these mountains well enough to know that only a fool would be wandering around on them after dark.

"Look," said Vanessa, still in the same even tone. "Here's where I think we are on the map. Remember how we went up and down that sharp ridge only about a quarter mile back? I think this is it on the map. At that point my compass read SSE. If we find this streambed," she added, pointing to a depression on the map, "within the next half mile, we'll know we're going the right way. If not, we'll stop then. What do you say?"

Naomi knew Vanessa, who had been hiking just as long as she had, was good with a map. Up to this point, she had always trusted her with a compass, too. She wanted to give in, but her heart pounded out two beats of fear that spelled *no*.

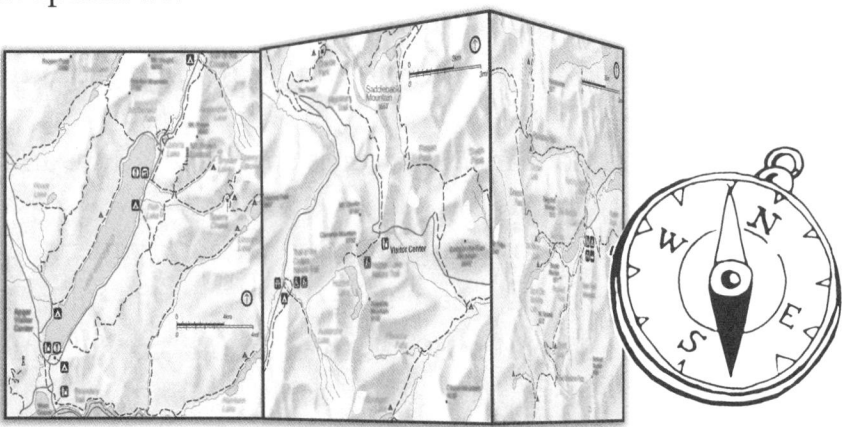

50 Lesson 6 — Comparison and Contrast

© The Continental Press, Inc. Do not duplicate.

Reading the Question

In this part of the lesson, you will see how one student, Hannah, used the details from the passage to write an answer to a test question.

> Sisters and brothers share many of the same traits, but they are different, too. Naomi and Vanessa must make a decision together. How will their similarities and their differences help them decide what to do? Write an essay describing how the girls are alike and how they are different. Finish your essay by telling what you think they will do and why.
>
> In your essay, include details from the story that show
> - ways the two characters are alike
> - ways they are different
> - how you decided what you think they will do

Hannah underlined important words in the question:

- Naomi and Vanessa
- alike and different
- what you think they will do
- details from the story

Hannah knew that she would be writing a comparison and contrast that her teacher and classmates would read.

Hannah spent about three minutes reading the question. She had to make sure she knew what the question was asking before she began to write. If Hannah had been confused by the question, she would have kept rereading until she understood it well.

Finish Line Writing 51

Planning to Write

The next step after reading the question is coming up with ideas. When you are sure you have correctly identified the two subjects for comparison and contrast, you should use a graphic organizer. This can be a two-column chart, a Venn diagram, or another organizer. Hannah created the Venn diagram below.

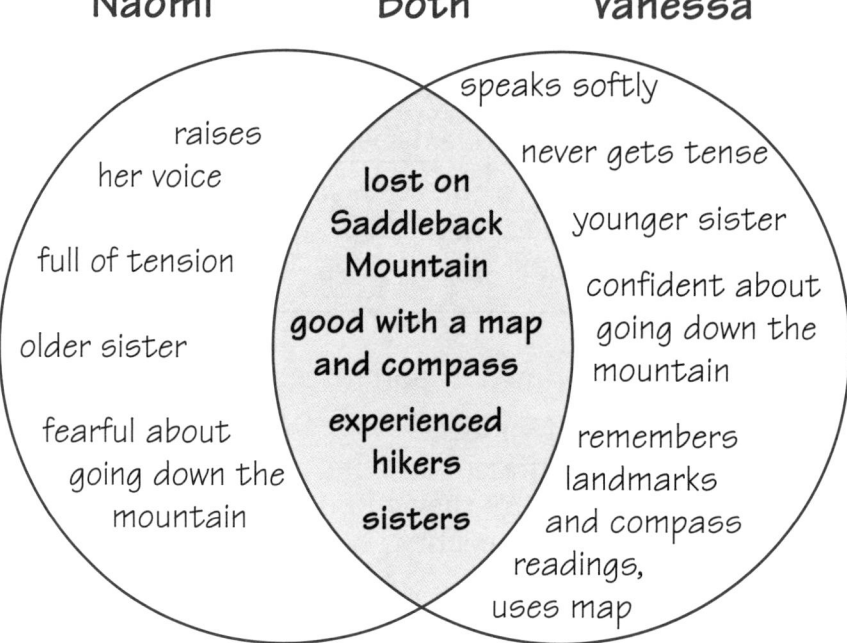

Completing the Plan

The next step is to organize your comparison-contrast writing into paragraphs. Hannah organized her writing into three paragraphs. Her first paragraph will tell how her characters are alike. The second paragraph will tell how they are different. In the third paragraph she will tell what she thinks they will do.

Help Hannah organize her first two paragraphs. Draw a line from each detail to the paragraph in which it fits. The first one has been done for you.

Paragraph 1:
Naomi and Vanessa are alike.

Naomi raises her voice, but Vanessa speaks softly.

They are lost on Saddleback Mountain.

They are good with a map and compass.

Naomi is tense, while Vanessa stays calm.

They are experienced hikers.

Paragraph 2:
Naomi and Vanessa are different.

Naomi is fearful about going down the mountain, but Vanessa is confident.

Naomi is two years older than Vanessa.

The girls are sisters.

Lesson 6 — Comparison and Contrast

Drafting

Writing a Draft

The next step is to use your graphic organizer or paragraph plan to write your draft. Begin each paragraph with a topic sentence. It should state the subjects you are comparing and contrasting. This is Hannah's draft.

  As sisters, Naomi and Vanessa are alike. They enjoy the outdoors. They love hiking. As experienced hikers, both of them are good with reading a map. They are also good with using a compass. In this story, however, despite their hiking experience, they are lost together on Saddleback mountain.

  Naomi and Vanessa are also different. Naomi is tense. She is afraid of going down the mountain. When she speaks, she raises her voice. And shows her fear. Vanessa is calm. She seems to be in control of the situation. She's confident about going down the mountain safely. Even though she is the younger sister. She uses the map, her compass and logical thinking to describe the situation. From the passage, you don't find out what happens in the next scene of the story, though.

  Even though Naomi is scared, I think they go down the mountain because Vanessa is confident. And she has a plan. She remembers passing the stream bed marked on they're map. She believes that if they fine it then they will know that they're going in the right direction. Naomi will probably follow Vanessa's lead.

1. Circle these transitions: *alike, both, different, even though.*

2. Underline the topic sentence in each paragraph.

3. List details in Paragraph 1: _____

4. List details in Paragraph 2: _____

5. List details in Paragraph 3: _____

Revising and Proofreading

Here is how Hannah revised her draft. Read the revision and answer the questions.

Revising

As sisters, Naomi and Vanessa are alike ^in many ways. They enjoy the outdoors. They love hiking. As experienced hikers, both of them are good with reading a map ~~They are also good~~ ^and with using a compass. In this story, however, despite their hiking experience, they are lost together on Saddleback mountain.

^In many ways Naomi and Vanessa are also different. Naomi is tense. ^In a scene from the story, She is afraid of going down the mountain. When she speaks, she raises her voice. ~~And~~ shows her fear. ^In contrast, Vanessa is calm. She seems to be in control of the situation. She's confident about going down the mountain safely. (Even though she is the younger sister.) She uses the map, her compass, and logical thinking to describe the situation. ~~From the passage, you don't find out what happens in the next scene of the story, though.~~

Even though Naomi is scared, I think they ^will go down the mountain because Vanessa is confident. ~~And~~ she has a plan. She remembers passing the stream-bed marked on they're map. She believes that if they fine it then they will know that they're going in the right direction. ^So Naomi will probably follow Vanessa's lead.

1. Which sentence did Hannah take out? _____

2. Underline the sentences she combined in the first paragraph.

3. Find two sentences in the first paragraph to combine. Correct the draft and write the revised sentence here.

_____

Proofreading Proofread Hannah's paper for three more mistakes. Write your corrections above.

Your Turn to Read

Now it's your turn to practice writing a comparison and contrast for a test. The first step in this process is to read about two subjects.

Franklin, Benjamin   Born in Boston in 1706, Benjamin Franklin moved to Philadelphia in 1723 to work as a printer. He published a newspaper, *Poor Richard's Almanack,* and his own autobiography. Franklin's talents went well beyond printing and writing, however. He sold books, established a library, and helped organize the first firefighting company in America. Franklin was also a great inventor. He is best remembered for his experiments with electricity, which led to his inventing the lightning rod. He also invented bifocals and a new kind of stove called the Franklin stove. Franklin is also remembered as a patriot and a revolutionary leader. He helped draft the Declaration of Independence, which he signed. He served the new American nation as minister to France and as its first postmaster. He was also a delegate to the Constitutional Convention and helped to make sure that the Constitution was ratified.

Jefferson, Thomas   Born in Virginia in 1743, Thomas Jefferson made the state his lifelong home. A patriot of the American Revolution, Jefferson was a leader in seeking American independence from Great Britain. He was on the committee that drafted the Declaration of Independence and is credited today as its author and one of its most famous signers. He became the governor of Virginia. He also served the new American nation as minister to France. He was in France when the Constitution was written, but he still worked to make sure it was ratified. In 1796, Jefferson became vice president of the United States. In 1800, he became the nation's third president. One of his great accomplishments in office was the Louisiana Purchase. Jefferson was much more than a patriot and statesman, however. He was also a scientist, a philosopher, and an architect. He designed his own home, Monticello, as well as the University of Virginia, which he helped to found.

Your Turn to Read the Question

Begin by reading the test question carefully. Underline important parts of the question. Then answer the questions.

> Two of the greatest leaders in the early history of our nation were Thomas Jefferson and Benjamin Franklin. Write an essay comparing and contrasting them. Then tell which man you think was more important to America and why you think so.
>
> In your essay, be sure to include details that show
> - ways the two men were alike
> - ways they were different
> - your reason for choosing who was more important

1. What is the topic of your essay?

_____

_____

2. What kind of writing are you being asked to do?

_____

_____

3. How will you structure your essay?

_____

_____

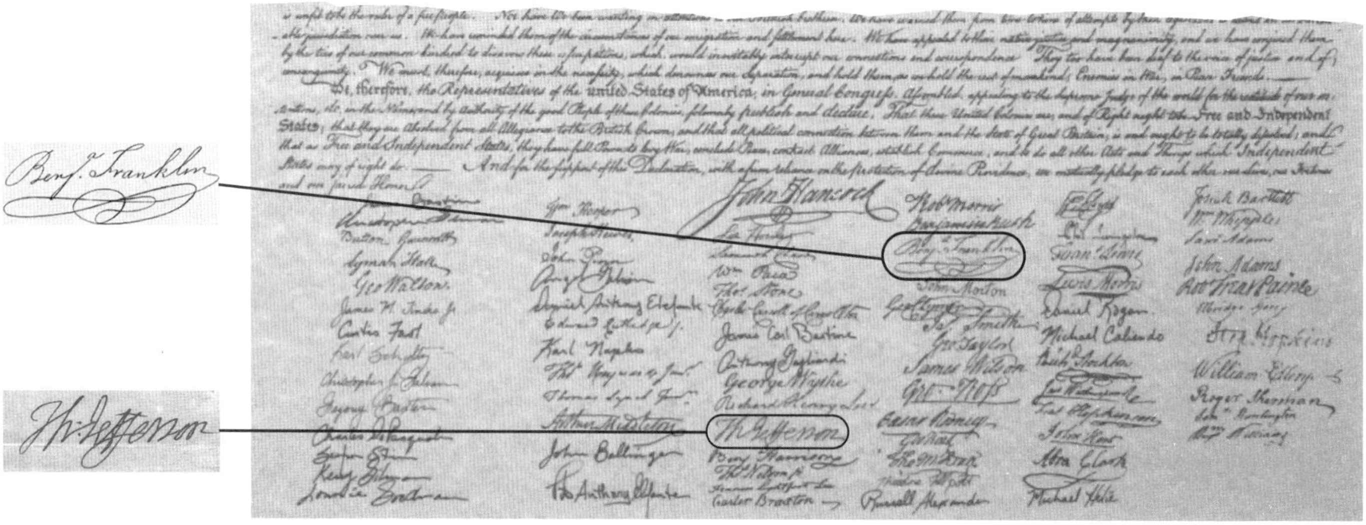

Lesson 6 — Comparison and Contrast

Your Turn to Plan
To plan your essay, use the Venn diagram below.

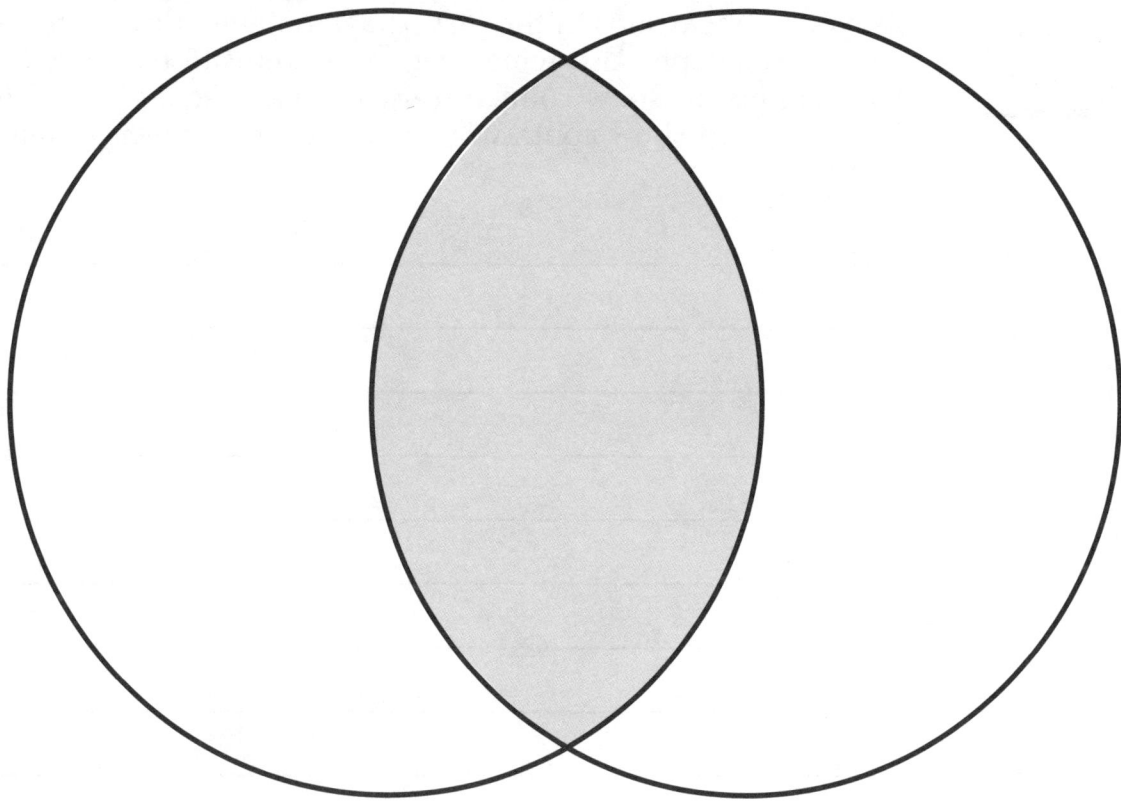

List ideas from your Venn diagram that you will put in each paragraph.

Paragraph 1

- _____
- _____
- _____
- _____

Paragraph 2

- _____
- _____
- _____
- _____

Paragraph 3

- _____
- _____
- _____
- _____

Your Turn to Write a Draft

Use your Venn diagram and your paragraph plans to help you as you write your draft. Be sure you begin each paragraph with a topic sentence. Then list your comparisons in the first paragraph and your contrasts in the second paragraph. Also remember to use transitional words and phrases. For example, to show comparisons, you can use *and, alike, like, also,* and *in addition.* To show contrast, you can use *but, different, unlike, however,* and *in contrast.*

_____
_____
_____
_____
_____
_____
_____
_____
_____
_____
_____
_____
_____
_____
_____
_____
_____
_____
_____

When you have finished your draft, go back over it. Make your revisions on this page. Proofread your draft. Then write your final answer on your own paper.

Your Turn to Score Writing

Use this rubric to review your own writing. Then exchange your paper with another student. Review each other's writing, and give it a score based on this rubric. Discuss ways you can each improve your writing.

Rubric for Writing Comparison and Contrast

Score 3
- The writing answers all parts of the test question.
- There are at least two clear comparisons and two clear contrasts.
- Transitional words and phrases connect the ideas.
- Each paragraph has a topic sentence that clearly states the subject.
- Supporting details are organized in a logical order.
- The writing is easy to read and stays on the subject.
- There are almost no mistakes in grammar, capitalization, punctuation, and spelling.

Score 2
- The writing answers almost all parts of the test question.
- There are two generally clear comparisons and contrasts.
- Transitional words and phrases connect most ideas.
- A topic sentence stating the subject is missing or unclear.
- Some supporting details are missing or are not in a logical order.
- The writing is fairly easy to read and mostly stays on the subject.
- There are some mistakes in grammar, capitalization, punctuation, and spelling.

Score 1
- The writing answers only part of the test question.
- There are fewer than two comparisons or two contrasts.
- Very few transitional words and phrases are used to connect ideas.
- More than one topic sentence is missing or unclear.
- Many supporting details are missing or are not in a logical order.
- The writing is not easy to read or is off the subject in many places.
- There are several mistakes in grammar, capitalization, punctuation, and spelling.

Lesson 7
Opinions and Facts

Does your town or city have a dog park? Do some people want to build one? What are the facts about dog parks? Read the question-and-answer article below to find out.

Questions and Answers About Dog Parks

Q. What is a dog park?
A. A dog park is a place where dogs can run off the leash and play with other dogs. A dog park can be fenced or unfenced. It can be the size of a house lot or many acres. It can be an official place—created just for dogs—or it can be a place where a lot of people have ended up taking their dogs unofficially.

Q. Why do some people want dog parks?
A. Most towns and cities have leash laws. As a result, most dogs do not get enough exercise. Some of them never have a chance to run free. In some cases, people let their dogs off the leash anyway. These dogs can scare children and do damage to property. Sometimes they even harm people.

Q. Are all dog parks run by cities and towns?
A. Some dog parks are public places: the town or city government runs them. Some are private. That means a few individuals get together to create a park. In these cases, only some dogs can enter, or people may have to pay a fee for their dog to use the park.

Q. Why are some people against dog parks?
A. Towns and cities typically have many improvements to make. These may include safe streets, new fire engines, more books for the library, and improvements to the schools. Some people say it is a waste of taxpayer money to build parks for dogs.

Q. What are the advantages of having a town or city dog park?
A. Pet owners are usually happier. They have a place to meet other dog owners. Sometimes, they get more exercise by taking their pets to the park. Sometimes, people without dogs are happier, too, because people aren't letting their dogs off the leash in the wrong places anymore, such as in children's play areas, sandboxes, and sports fields.

Reading the Question

In this part of the lesson, you will see how one student, Carlos, used the facts from the article to write an answer to a test question.

Carlos began by reading the test question carefully.

> Does your town or city need a dog park? If it already has a dog park, should it have a bigger dog park or more dog parks? Write an article for your neighborhood newsletter that states your opinion for or against a dog park in your town or city.
>
> Be sure to do the following:
> - include a topic sentence that clearly states your opinion
> - support your opinion with at least three good reasons or facts
> - write for adults in your city or town who will take part in making the decision

When Carlos read the question, he made notes to himself:

My subject—a dog park in my town

What I have to write—an article

My audience—adults who will help decide on the change

What I have to do—state my opinion and back it up with at least three good reasons or facts

 Carlos spent about three minutes reading the test question. He made sure he knew exactly what it was asking before he began to plan his response.

Finish Line Writing

Planning to Write

The next step is to decide on your opinion. Then use a graphic organizer to make sure you state both an opinion and some reasons and facts that support it. Here is the organizer Carlos used.

Prewriting

My Opinion: Bridgewater needs a dog park.
Reason/Fact 1: We have a leash law, so dogs can't run free.
Reason/Fact 2: They need to get exercise and they need a safe place to play with other dogs.
Reason/Fact 3: Some people in our town break the law—they take their dogs to the park and let them off the leash. This scares some little kids.
Reason/Fact 4: Sometimes the dogs make messes in the park, too.
Reason/Fact 5:
Conclusion: We need it for the town.

Completing the Plan

Add a fifth reason or fact to Carlos's graphic organizer.

Lesson 7 — Opinions and Facts

Writing a Draft

The next step is to use your graphic organizer or paragraph plan to write your draft. This is Carlos's draft.

Drafting

　　The City of Bridgewater should have a dog park. The first reason for this is that we have a leash law. Dogs need exercise, and most of them cant get enough exercise when there on a leash or tied up in a backyard. The perfect place for a dog to run free is a dog park.

　　Second, we need a special place for dogs to run free a place where they won't bother people. Sometimes, people take their dogs to the park and let them off of the leash. It sometimes scares little kids. I know one little girl on my street that is really, really scared of dogs. Sometimes, the dogs make messes that their owners don't clean up, this ruins parks for people. This is against the law. We need a special place for dogs so people can have clean parks for themself. And have parks where their children feel safe.

　　Finally, dog parks are good for people too. At dog parks, dog owners meet other dog owners. They become friends with people who share there own interests. Building a dog park is one way to show that we understand. Building a dog park is for people in our city who have diffrent needs.

In the paragraphs above, circle these transitions: *first, second,* and *finally.* Tell how this test answer is organized by identifying the following:

Topic Sentence/Opinion: _____

Fact/Reason 1: _____

Fact/Reason 2: _____

Fact/Reason 3: _____

Revising and Proofreading

Here is how Carlos revised his draft. Read the revision and answer the questions below.

Revising

The City of Bridgewater should have a dog park. The first reason for this is that we have a leash law. ^*in our city, so dogs cannot run free* Dogs need exercise, and most of them can't get enough exercise when ~~there~~ *they're* on a leash or tied up in a backyard. The perfect place for a dog to run free is a dog park *with a fence*.

Second, we need a special place for dogs to run free a place where they won't bother people. Sometimes, people take their dogs to the park and let them off of the leash. It sometimes scares *children* ~~little kids~~. ~~I know one little girl on my street that is really, really scared of dogs.~~ Sometimes, the dogs make messes that their owners don't clean up. this ruins parks for people. (This is against the law.) We need a special place for dogs so people can have clean parks for themself. ~~And have parks~~ where their children feel safe.

Finally, dog parks are good for people, too. At dog parks, dog owners meet other dog owners. They become friends with people who share there own interests. Building a dog park is one way to show that we understand ~~Building a dog park is for~~ people in our city ~~who~~ have diffrent needs.

1. Why did Carlos add the words *with a fence* to the last sentence in paragraph one? _____

_____

2. Underline a run-on sentence in the second paragraph that needs to be corrected. Correct the sentence and write it on your own paper.

Proofreading   Proofread Carlos's paper for four more mistakes. Write your corrections above.

Lesson 7 — Opinions and Facts

Your Turn to Read

Now it's your turn to practice writing an opinion and facts for a test. The first step in this process is to read about an issue.

A Difference Over Goals

Shawsville, IN 6/24/05 The people of Shawsville are divided over the issue of land.

In the past two weeks, signs have gone up all over town. Some say things like "More Soccer Fields for Shawsville!" and "We Just Want to Play Soccer." Others say "Let's Save Our Land" and "No More Soccer Fields."

People on both sides get a bit excited when you ask them their opinion. This small town has more than 900 children who play soccer, yet it has only three fields. Two of them are at the regional high school and, therefore, sometimes in use by the high school team.

Soccer moms and dads are angry that their children can't play every Saturday and often can't practice more than once a week. They propose building two new fields on the Greenway Conservation Land. They point to a flat meadow that is not far from the parking area. They say it could easily be turned into much needed fields. "Then the children will be happy," they say. They add that playing soccer is excellent exercise and helps their children stay fit.

Some people in Shawsville see the issue very differently, however. "That's conservation land!" they say. They quickly add, "Using that land is against the law!"

They are correct: the town of Shawsville will need, among other legal requirements, to have a special two-thirds vote to use the land. Then there's the cost of building the fields and adding more parking.

The town budget is already strained from last year's addition to the police station. Some people say Shawsville can't afford the project and won't be able to maintain it. Others say that if money is going to be spent, it should be spent adding a classroom to the overcrowded elementary school.

Your Turn to Read the Question

Your next step is to read the test question carefully. Underline important parts of the test question. Then answer the questions that follow.

> All over the country, more children than ever are playing soccer, lacrosse, and other sports. Many communities find they do not have enough sports fields. Imagine that your town or city does not have enough playing fields for all the children who want to play sports. Should your community build a new field? If so, will it be a problem to find the land? Write an article that states your opinion for or against a new sports field.
>
> Be sure to do the following:
> - include a topic sentence that clearly states your opinion
> - support your opinion with at least three good reasons or facts
> - write for your local newspaper, which will be read by many members of your community

1. What kind of writing are you being asked to do?

   _____

   _____

2. How will your writing be structured when you are done?

   _____

   _____

3. Who is your audience?

   _____

   _____

4. How much time should you spend reading this test question?

   _____

   _____

Lesson 7 — Opinions and Facts

Your Turn to Plan

Use this opinion and reasons/facts organizer to plan your article. Add reasons/facts as needed.

My Opinion:
Reason/Fact 1:

Your Turn to Write a Draft

Use your organizer to help you as you write your draft. Be sure you begin your paragraph with a topic sentence. Then state and explain each fact or reason. Remember to link your ideas with transitions. These can include words like *and, also,* and *in addition.* They should also include words that show the order and importance of your facts and reasons, such as *first, second, next, finally, last,* and *most important.*

___

When you have finished your draft, go back over it. Make your revisions on this page. Proofread your draft. Then write your final answer on your own paper.

Your Turn to Score Writing

Use this rubric to review your own writing. Then exchange your paper with another student. Review each other's writing, and give it a score based on this rubric. Discuss ways you can each improve your writing.

Rubric for Writing Opinions and Facts

Score 3
- The writing answers all parts of the test question.
- The ideas are clear, and appropriate transitions connect them.
- Each paragraph has a topic sentence that clearly states the subject.
- Facts and reasons are clear and are in a logical order.
- The writing is easy to read and stays on the subject.
- Words are used correctly and well.
- There are almost no mistakes in grammar, capitalization, punctuation, and spelling.

Score 2
- The writing answers almost all parts of the test question.
- The ideas are mostly clear, and transitions connect most of them.
- A topic sentence stating the subject is missing or unclear.
- Some facts and reasons are unclear or are not in a logical order.
- The writing is fairly easy to read and mostly stays on the subject.
- Some words are misused.
- There are some mistakes in grammar, capitalization, punctuation, and spelling.

Score 1
- The writing answers only part of the test question.
- The ideas are not clear, or they are not connected.
- A topic sentence stating the subject is missing or unclear.
- Most of the facts and reasons are unclear or are not in a logical order.
- The writing is not easy to read or is off the subject in many places.
- Many words are overused or misused.
- There are several mistakes in grammar, capitalization, punctuation, and spelling.

Lesson 8 Writing Sentences

A sentence has two parts: a subject and a predicate. The key word in the subject is the **simple subject.** It is a noun or pronoun. The key word in the predicate is the **simple predicate.** It is a verb or verb phrase. A verb phrase includes the main verb and any helping verbs.

Agreement

In order for a sentence to be correct, the subject and verb must agree in number. That means that if the subject is singular, the verb must be singular. If the subject is plural, the verb must be plural. Remember, singular means one; plural means more than one. In the following examples, each subject is underlined once, and each verb is underlined twice.

Singular The horse pulls the wagon.

Plural Two horses pull the plow.

Generally, singular verbs in the present tense end in *s* or *es*.

Singular The student finishes her homework.

Plural verbs in the present tense do not end in *s* or *es*.

Plural The students finish their homework.

However, if the singular subject is *I* or *you,* this rule does not apply. The verb does not end in *s* or *es*.

Singular I finish my homework.

Compound Subjects

A **compound subject** is two or more simple subjects joined by *and* or *or*. A compound subject and its verb must also agree in number. When the subjects are joined by *and,* the verb is plural. This is true whether the subjects themselves are singular or plural.

Two Singular Subjects Los Angeles *and* San Francisco are in California.

Two Plural Subjects Apples *and* oranges are popular fruits.

Compound Predicates

A **compound predicate** is two or more simple predicates joined by *and* or *or*. The verbs in a compound predicate must agree in number with the subject.

Singular The airplane makes a loud roar *and* rises off the ground.

Plural The freshly baked cookies smell great *and* taste good.

A. In each sentence, circle the correct verb in parentheses.

1. Many children (likes, like) to play video games.
2. Some children (use, uses) the computer for sending e-mail.
3. Computers (are, is) a very useful tool for learning in the classroom.
4. A young child easily (learn, learns) to use a mouse.
5. Keyboards (takes, take) a longer time to master.
6. Word games and video games (is, are) fun to play on the computer.
7. Libraries (have, has) computers available for Internet searches.

B. In each sentence, circle the correct subject in parentheses.

1. The (river, rivers) flows right near my house.
2. Beautiful (flowers, flower) grow along the banks of the river.
3. The (neighbor, neighbors) sometimes join us for a swim.
4. The (rock, rocks) are sometimes slippery.
5. My (leg, legs) has a bruise from the last time I fell in the water.
6. My (friend, friends) were worried that I would drown.

C. Complete each of the following sentences by writing the correct present tense form of the verb(s) in parentheses.

1. Jared's grandfather _____ clocks. (fix)
2. Jared _____ to learn how to fix them, too. (want)
3. Clocks _____ sometimes run by gears. (be)
4. The teeth in the gears _____ worn out and _____ to be repaired. (get) (need)
5. Jared's sister _____ it's fun to learn about clocks. (think)

Finish Line Writing

Subject Pronouns

A pronoun is a word that takes the place of a noun. A pronoun that replaces a subject is called a **subject pronoun**.

Subject Pronouns	
Singular	Plural
I	we
you	you
he, she, it	they

By using pronouns in your writing, you can replace a noun and avoid repeating it. Notice how the second pair of sentences sounds better by replacing the subject *Sean* with the subject pronoun *he*.

Every morning, **Sean** delivers the paper. **Sean** never misses a delivery!

Every morning, **Sean** delivers the paper. **He** never misses a delivery!

In compound subjects that include the pronoun *I,* it is important to follow this rule: Always name yourself last, after all the other nouns or pronouns making up the compound subject.

Incorrect   I, **Vincent**, and **Miguel** plan to go to the game together.

Correct   **Vincent, Miguel**, and I plan to go to the game together.

Agreement

When replacing a noun with a pronoun, the pronoun must agree with the noun in **number**. This simply means that if a noun is singular, the pronoun must be singular. If the noun is plural, then the pronoun must be plural.

Singular   **Houston** is located near the Gulf of Mexico.
    It is a busy seaport.

Plural   The **cheerleaders** practice after school.
    They perform at all of the football games.

Besides agreeing with a noun in number, a pronoun must also agree in **gender.** Like nouns, pronouns can be masculine, feminine, or neuter in gender. Look at the box above. Write which subject pronoun is

Masculine: _____   Feminine: _____   Neuter: _____

Masculine   **Silvio** is a new student.
    He is in Lucy's math class.

Feminine   **Lucy** helps out in the library.
    She volunteers on Mondays.

Neuter   The new **atlas** is finally here.
    It will be a good reference book.

Lesson 8 — Writing Sentences

A. In each sentence, underline the subject noun. On the line at the right, write the correct pronoun to replace the noun.

1. Charles wants a clarinet for his birthday. _____
2. The concert was a huge success. _____
3. The blizzard left six inches of snow on the ground. _____
4. My brother and I always stretch after our run. _____
5. The old coins are very valuable. _____
6. Sarah does not like folk music. _____
7. Whales and dolphins are mammals. _____

B. In each sentence or pair of sentences, write the correct pronoun on the line provided.

1. The boys ran to the bus stop, but _____ missed the bus.
2. Corinne and I read about sharks. _____ drew pictures of them.
3. Running water causes erosion. _____ wears away rocks and soil.
4. Vitamins are important. _____ should be part of a balanced diet.
5. The skaters practiced on the ice, so _____ would perform well.
6. Daniel forgot to set his alarm this morning, so _____ was late for school.
7. Carl and Linda painted the fence. He liked painting it, but _____ didn't.

C. Rewrite each incorrect sentence using the correct pronoun.

1. Clara Barton was a nurse. He helped soldiers wounded in battle.

   _____

2. When snow melts, they runs downhill.

   _____

3. Harriet Tubman was born enslaved, but they helped other slaves to escape to freedom.

   _____

4. Machu Picchu is sometimes called the city in the clouds. They was built about 550 years ago.

   _____

Finish Line Writing **73**

Object Pronouns

A pronoun that replaces a direct object or an object of a preposition is an **object pronoun**. A direct object is the object of a verb. It receives the direct action of the verb. An object of a preposition is a word that is used after prepositions such as *to, for, in, at,* and *with,* to name a few.

Direct Objects	Eva joined her **friends** in a game of soccer.
	Eva joined **them** in a game of soccer.
Objects of Prepositions	Hector threw the ball to **Andrew**.
	Hector threw the ball to **him**.

An object pronoun can be singular or plural, depending on the noun it replaces. The chart below will help you compare subject pronouns and object pronouns in both their singular and plural forms.

	Subject Pronouns	Object Pronouns
Singular	I	me
	you	you
	he, she, it	him, her, it
Plural	we	us
	you	you
	they	them

In compound objects that include the pronoun *me*, it is important to follow this rule: Always name yourself last, after all the other nouns or pronouns making up the compound object.

Here are examples of compound direct objects.

Incorrect	The dog followed **me** and Len.
Correct	The dog followed Len and **me**.

Here are examples of compound objects of a preposition.

Incorrect	The package was addressed to **me** and Sally.
Correct	The package was addressed to Sally and **me**.

A. Write a sentence for each of the following.

1. Compound direct objects: _____

_____

2. Compound objects of a preposition: _____

_____

Lesson 8 — Writing Sentences

A. In each sentence, underline the direct object or object of a preposition. On the line at the right, replace the noun with the correct pronoun.

1. The coach asked José and Steven to play. _____
2. The bus stopped for Emily. _____
3. Mrs. Sanchez talked to John yesterday. _____
4. The wind blew the paper away. _____
5. The clown smiled at Paul. _____

B. In each sentence, circle the correct pronoun in parentheses.

1. The toll collector took money from (we, us).
2. The Statue of Liberty fascinated (they, them).
3. The teacher allowed (he, him) to take a different test.
4. The flowers made (she, her) think of spring.
5. (He, Him) entered the room and the cat followed (he, him).
6. Emily and (she, her) showed pictures of their trip to Scott and (I, me).

Possessive Nouns and Pronouns

A **possessive noun** shows ownership. A noun can be made to show ownership by changing its form.

Noun   A picture of my **family** is on the desk.

Possessive My **family's** picture is on the desk.
Noun

Singular Nouns

To make a singular noun possessive add an apostrophe and an -s.

Hilda's gloves are on the table.

Mrs. **Kass's** tulips were blooming.

Plural Nouns

To make a plural noun that ends in s possessive add an apostrophe only.

The **students'** reports were on display.

The **Smiths'** house was being painted.

Finish Line Writing

To make a plural noun that does not end in *s* a possessive noun, add an apostrophe and an *-s*.

> The **children's** notebooks were collected for review.
> The **mice's** footsteps could be heard.

Sometimes it can be hard to tell if a word is a possessive noun or a plural noun just by hearing the word spoken. For example, *teachers, teacher's,* and *teachers'* all sound the same. However, by looking at the spelling of the word and the way the word is used in a sentence, you can determine what it is.

Plural Noun	The **teachers** are meeting today.
Singular Possessive Noun	The **teacher's** meeting is today.
Plural Possessive Noun	The **teachers'** meeting is today.

Possessive Pronouns

Possessive pronouns are pronouns that show possession or ownership of something. Just as subject pronouns replace nouns as subjects, possessive pronouns replace nouns that show possession.

Possessive Noun   Miranda washed **Miranda's** dishes.
Possessive Pronoun   Miranda washed **her** dishes.

Possessive Pronouns	
Singular	Plural
my	our
mine	ours
your	your
yours	yours
his	their
her	theirs
hers	
its	

Some of these possessive pronouns are always used with nouns. Others always stand alone, which means nouns do not follow them.

Pronouns used with nouns: *my, your, his, her, its, our, their*

> Have you seen **my** notebook?
> **Her** blue jacket is on the chair.
> Sara came to **our** house today.

Pronouns that stand alone: *mine, yours, his, hers, its, ours, theirs*

> I think that notebook is **mine.**
> This is my blue jacket. **Hers** is on the chair.
> First we went to Sara's house then we went to **ours.**

Lesson 8 — Writing Sentences

A. In each sentence, write the possessive form of the noun in parentheses on the line provided.

1. The _____ croaking was very loud. (frog)
2. The _____ wings are used for flight. (birds)
3. The _____ trophies were on display. (winners)
4. The _____ hat blew off in the gust of wind. (woman)
5. The _____ performance pleased the crowd. (band)
6. The _____ house is newly painted. (Joneses)

B. Replace each underlined group of words with a possessive noun.

1. the chalk belonging to the teacher _____
2. the whistles belonging to the coaches _____
3. the jacket worn by Mr. Gross _____
4. the dew drops on the leaves _____
5. the books belonging to the children _____

C. In each sentence, underline the possessive noun(s). On the line at the right, replace the possessive noun(s) with the correct possessive pronoun.

1. The winning poster is Mike's and Todd's. _____
2. The library's books are on the shelves. _____
3. The remaining piece of pizza is Brian's. _____
4. Erin's sneakers were covered with mud. _____
5. He used blue paint for the children's room. _____

D. In each sentence, circle the correct pronoun in parentheses.

1. The road sign fell down last night and hit (him, his) car.
2. George and (I, me) will rake the leaves off the lawn.
3. (We, Us) are practicing for the spelling bee.
4. Will Amy and (she, her) finish (her, their) project on time?
5. Could these books be (theirs, their's)?

Finish Line Writing

Your Turn to Edit

A. Edit the paragraph below to correct possessive nouns, subject pronouns, object pronouns, possessive pronouns, and subject-verb agreement. Cross out each mistake and write the correction above it.

Beth knows that ants is fascinating to watch, so he decides to build an ant farm. Beths' friends wants to help. They ask she what materials to use. Beth tells they to gather the things on hers list. Her will supervise the building of the ant farm with the friend's materials. Beth and her friends researches ants to learn more about it. The friends or Beth plan to make a poster about ants. The girl's research has taught them that ants live in colonies, and different kinds of ants has different jobs. The queen lays eggs. She is larger than the other ants. Worker ants take care of she. Soldier ants protect the colony. Beth and her friends also learn that some ants bite. Beth tells her friends, "Me and you will have to be careful! Us don't want to get bitten!"

Lesson 8 — Writing Sentences

B. To edit the paragraph below for subject-verb agreement, circle the correct verb form in parentheses. Then edit to correct possessive nouns, subject pronouns, object pronouns, and possessive pronouns. Cross out each mistake and write the correction above it.

Although Andrews mother (tell, tells) he it is not a good idea to bring his computer to school, him (does, do) so anyway. At school he (try, tries) to be very careful, but he accidentally (bumps, bump) into the table and (knock, knocks) the computer onto the floor. Her friends (gasps, gasp) when it falls. The teacher (hope, hopes) that the fall hasn't broken its. Although it (seems, seem) fine, the screen (remain, remains) dark. Andrew is very worried. Then one of his friends (call, calls) to him from across the room. "Look!" he (exclaims, exclaim). "The screens' cord is unplugged." Andrew (plug, plugs) in the cord, and the computer (come, comes) to life. He tells him friends, "Now me and you can do our work."

Lesson 9: Writing a Narrative

Narrative writing tells a story with a clear beginning, middle, and end. A **personal narrative** is based on events that happened to the writer over a short period of time. A personal narrative might be about the first time you met a cousin or a time you were frightened. You write a personal narrative in the first person, using the pronouns *I* and *me*.

A **creative narrative** is a story that has been made up. Short stories and novels are creative narratives. Even though the plot is made up, writers usually use details and information from real life to make their stories come alive for readers.

The details of a narrative should usually be in the order they happened. A narrative should also be set in a particular time and place, called the **setting**. The time might be "yesterday" or "once upon a time." The place could be your classroom or outer space. The last sentences of a narrative should pull the story together.

Here is a question that asks you to write a personal narrative.

> Write a story for your class about a time you had to go to the doctor.
> - Choose one specific visit when something interesting happened.
> - Arrange your details in time order.
> - Be sure to include clues to the setting.
> - Write three paragraphs.

Reading the Question

Here is how one student, Tasha, approached the test question. She began by reading the question carefully. The word *story* gave her a clue that told her she would be writing a narrative. The words *clues to the setting* meant that she would have to tell readers when and where the story happened.

Then, she read the question once more. The words *Choose one specific visit* told her the narrative should be about one event. The words *Arrange your details in time order* let her know she should start with what happened first, then tell each detail in the order it happened.

Tasha spent about three minutes reading the test question. She made sure she understood exactly what it was asking before she began planning what to write.

Planning to Write

The next step is to make a plan of what you will write. The right graphic organizer can help you put your ideas in order. You should choose a graphic organizer that fits the kind of writing you need to do.

In this case, the test question asked Tasha to write a story about an event in her life with the details arranged in time order. She chose a chart to help her collect the details of her story and put them in time order.

Prewriting

Subject: My Last Visit to Doctor Smith's Office
Time Order (Chronological Order)
1 Nipper got out of the backyard; broke my pinky while chasing after him
2 scared on the way to Dr. Smith's; I was sad about losing Nipper
3
4
5
6
7

Completing the Plan

What do you think happened next? Look at the items below and number them in the time order in which you think they happened.

    I heard a strange yelping sound at Dr. Smith's.

    Nipper was there!

    I wanted to get up and investigate the room the sound was coming from, but Mom wouldn't let me.

    I ran across the office toward the sound.

    I hugged Nipper as Dr. Smith put a splint on my pinky.

Writing a Draft

Once you've developed a plan for your writing, you will be ready to write your first draft. Don't worry about making your first draft perfect. The important thing is to write down your ideas. Here is Tasha's draft.

Drafting

My last visit to the doctor's office hapened when I broke my finger while chasing after Nipper. Nipper was my pupy, and she had gotten out of the backyard that morning. Her paw was hurt. I had no idea that my visit to Dr. Smith's office would be such an interesting one.

On the way to Dr. Smith's office, I was feeling scared because I didn't know what was going to hapen to my finger. I was also very sad about losing Nipper that morning. We were all sad about losing little Nipper. He was such a special member of our family.

When my mother and me walked into the doctor's office, I heard a yelping sound, like a howling. The sound made me forget about my finger. All I wanted to do was to get up and check out the room from which the sound was coming. My mother told me to just sit quietly and wait for the doctor, but I couldn't. The yelping was loud, so I ran. Across the office toward the sound. There was nipper! A man had brought her to Dr. Smith's because he had found her near by. I through my arms around Nipper and sat beside her. As Dr. Smith put a splint on my finger. I had no idea that my visit to Dr. Smith's office would end up reuniting me with Nipper!

1. What specific event does Tasha focus on? _____

_____

2. Circle the words or phrases that show time order.

Revising and Proofreading

The text below shows how Tasha revised her first draft. Keep your eyes open for errors that Tasha may have missed!

Revising

My last visit to the doctor's office hapened when I broke my finger while chasing after Nipper. Nipper was my pupy, and she had gotten out of the backyard that morning. ~~Her paw was hurt.~~ I had no idea that my visit to Dr. Smith's office would be such an interesting one.

On the way to Dr. Smith's office, I was feeling scared because I didn't know what was going to hapen to my finger. I was also very sad about losing Nipper that morning. ~~We were all sad about losing little Nipper.~~ **She** ~~He~~ was such a special member of our family.

When my mother and me walked into the doctor's office, I heard a yelping sound, like a **dog** howling. The **strange** sound made me forget about my finger. All I wanted to do was to get up and check out the room from which the sound was coming. My mother told me to just sit quietly and wait for the doctor, but I couldn't. The yelping was loud, so I ran. Across the office toward the sound. There was nipper! A man had brought her to Dr. Smith's because he had found her near by. I ~~through~~ **threw** my arms around Nipper and sat beside her. As Dr. Smith put a splint on my finger. I had no idea that my visit to Dr. Smith's office would end up reuniting me with Nipper!

1. What did Tasha do to revise the structure of her draft?

_____

2. Why did Tasha change *He* to *She*? *Through* to *threw*?

_____

Proofreading

Proofread Tasha's draft for five more errors. Make the corrections on the draft above.

Finish Line Writing

Your Turn to Read

Read the following newspaper article about a relay race. You will use information in the article to write a narrative.

On Your Marks, Get Set, Go!
Smith and Jones Lead the Eagles to Victory

Yesterday's girls' track meet brought the Eagles an unexpected victory over the Lions in the 400-meter relay category.

The rain poured down on the starting line as the runners, including Jennifer Smith of the Eagles and Maria Gonzalez of the Lions, listened hard for the sound of the gun. Bang! They were off! For an instant, Smith was in the lead. A second later, there was Gonzalez, inching closer. Smith, clearly running at full speed, looked pained as Gonzalez suddenly sped ahead. Time seemed to slow down as Gonzalez reached out to pass the baton to her teammate, Donna Chow. The stands were silent as Gonzalez's baton grazed Chow's hand and dropped to the ground!

Smith, only a second behind, successfully passed her baton on to Jones—one of the Eagles' fastest runners. There was no catching up for the Lions, and the Eagles soared to victory!

Jennifer Smith successfully passes the baton to Becky Jones during yesterday's meet.

1. What specific event is this narrative writing focused on?

_____

_____

2. What are some of the details and words that bring this story to life for readers?

_____

_____

_____

_____

Your Turn to Read the Question

Now it's your turn. Begin by reading the test question below carefully.

> Imagine that you were at the race. Write a narrative about the race based on the article. Write a personal narrative as if you were in the race or were an onlooker. In your narrative be sure to include
> - a plot or story told in time order
> - details that make the story realistic
> - a sense of the setting

1. What kind of writing are you being asked to do, and how do you know?

_____

_____

2. Who is your audience?

_____

Your Turn to Plan

Fill in this chart to help you answer the test question and to arrange your narrative's events in time order.

Subject:
Time Order (Chronological Order)
1
2
3
4
5
6

Your Turn to Write a Draft

Now it's your turn to write a draft. Before you begin, review your graphic organizer. Think about the main subject of your paragraphs. Is it specific enough? Are the supporting details listed in time order? Remember to use words that bring your story to life and make readers want to know what happens next.

_____
_____
_____
_____
_____
_____
_____
_____
_____
_____
_____
_____
_____
_____
_____
_____
_____
_____
_____
_____
_____
_____

When you have finished your draft, go back over it. Make your revisions on this page. Proofread your draft. Then write your final answer on your own paper.

Your Turn to Score Writing

Use this rubric to review your own paper. Then review another student's paper. Write your suggestions for ways the paper could be improved. Give the paper a score based on this rubric.

Rubric for Writing a Narrative

Score 3
- The writing answers all parts of the test question.
- The supporting details are in time order and relate directly to the main topic.
- The setting is clearly suggested.
- The concluding sentences sum up the preceding paragraphs and bring them to a close.
- Words are used correctly and well.
- There are almost no mistakes in grammar, capitalization, punctuation, and spelling.

Score 2
- The writing answers almost all parts of the test question.
- At least a few supporting details relate directly to the main topic and are in time order.
- The setting is not clear.
- The concluding sentences relate to the preceding paragraphs.
- Some words are misused.
- There are some mistakes in grammar, capitalization, punctuation, and spelling.

Score 1
- The writing answers only part of the test question.
- The supporting details do not relate directly to a main topic and are not in time order.
- The writer doesn't include a setting.
- The concluding sentences do not relate to the preceding paragraphs.
- Many words are overused or misused.
- There are several mistakes in grammar, capitalization, punctuation, and spelling.

Lesson 10 Informational Writing

Informational writing is what you do when you write a report or answer a question on a test. It is the kind of writing you do most often. Unlike narrative writing, informational writing should be factual, not personal or creative. It should be clear and direct. The reader should know right away what you are writing about.

Informational writing needs to be well organized so that readers can follow what you want to say. You can organize informational writing by main idea and detail, by cause and effect, by comparison and contrast, or by a sequence of steps.

Here is a test question that asks you to write directions. For directions you will want to think about a sequence of steps.

> You have been asked to write directions for younger students explaining how to use the computer to find information for a project. Write a paper with the directions you will give for searching the Web.
> - Be sure to put the steps in order and include all the steps that you usually follow.
> - Write two or more paragraphs.
> - Explain any terms you think readers won't be familiar with.

Reading the Question

Now you will see how one student, Daniel, approached the test question. Before he began to write, he read the question carefully. The word *directions* let him know he was going to have to explain a process, or how to do something. The words *steps* and *order* told him he would need to think about the sequence of steps he would follow to search for information on the Web.

Daniel read the question once more for clues about his audience and how to write his paper. The question reads: "You have been asked to write directions for younger students. . . ." Because he would be writing for younger students, his writing style would need to be simple and clear.

Daniel spent about three minutes reading the test question. He made sure he understood exactly what it was asking before he began to plan his response.

Planning to Write

The next step is to make a plan of what you will write. Graphic organizers can help you organize your thoughts. It's important to choose a graphic organizer that works well for the kind of writing you need to do. In this case, the test question asked Daniel to write about the process of finding information on the Web. He chose a sequence chart to help put his thoughts in order. Notice how he used transitional words like *first, next,* and *then.*

Prewriting

Looking up Information on the Web	
Step 1	First, choose a topic that you would like to learn more about.
Step 2	Next, using your computer, choose a search engine that will help you find websites about your topic. If you need help, you can ask a teacher or a librarian.
Step 3	Then, pick some key words about your topic.
Step 4	
Step 5	
Step 6	

Completing the Plan

Now it's your turn. Look at the items below and choose three to complete the sequence chart above. Label your choices *Step 4, Step 5,* and *Step 6* in that order. For the items that do not belong, leave the space blank. Then write your choices in the chart above.

Finally, choose a website that you want to read more about and click on it.

Next, type your key words into the search engine and press the return key.

Write out all of the results you do not want on a separate sheet of paper.

After you press the return key, you will see a list of websites about your topic.

Ask the librarian to help you turn on the computer.

Writing a Draft

Once you've developed a plan for your writing, you will be ready to write your first draft. Here is the draft Daniel wrote based on his sequence chart. As you read it, notice the transitional words he uses to lead from one idea to the next.

Drafting

Looking up information on the Web can sem confusing at first... sometimes it's hard to know where to begin. Here are some basic steps can follow to find the information you're looking for. Don't forget to make sure you have a good electrical connection.

First, choose a topic that you would like to learn more about. I like water and stars as topics. Next, using your computer, choose a search engine that will help find websites about your topic. If need help, you can ask a teacher or librarian. Then, pick some key words about your topic. Try to be as specific as you can. Next, type your key words into the search engine and the return key. Next, type your key words into the search engine and the return key. After you press the return key, you will see a list of wesites about your topic. Finally, chose a website that you want to read more and click on it. These basic steps will help you more easily locate the information you're looking for on the Web.

1. How did Daniel organize his directions? _____

2. Circle the transitional words in Daniel's draft.

Revising and Proofreading

The text below shows how Daniel revised his first draft. Keep your eyes open for errors that he may have missed!

Revising

Looking up information on the Web can sem confusing at first. ~~S~~sometimes it's hard to know where to begin. Here are some basic steps can follow to find the information you're looking for. ~~Don't forget to make sure you have a good electrical connection.~~

First, choose a topic that you would like to learn more about. ~~I like water and stars as topics.~~ Next, using your computer, choose a search engine that will help ^you^ find websites about your topic. If ^you^ need help, you can ask a teacher or librarian. Then, pick some key words about your topic. Try to be as specific as you can. Next, type your key words into the search engine and ^press^ the return key. Next, type your key words into the search engine and the return key. After you press the return key, you will see a list of wesites about your topic. Finally, chose a website that you want to read more and click on it. These basic steps will help you more easily locate the information you're looking for on the Web.

1. Why was the second sentence in the second paragraph deleted?

_____

2. Circle Daniel's concluding sentence. Why does it work well as a conclusion?

_____

Proofreading

Proofread Daniel's draft for five more errors. Write your corrections on his draft above.

Finish Line Writing 91

Your Turn to Read

Look at the time line below. You will use facts from this time line to do some informational writing.

The Life of Dr. Martin Luther King, Jr. (MLK)

1929
January 15 MLK is born in Atlanta, GA.

1935
September MLK begins school at an all-black elementary school in Atlanta, GA.

1944
June MLK enters Morehouse College in Atlanta.

1948
February MLK is ordained a Baptist minister. He enters the Crozer Theological Seminary in Chester, PA.

1953
June MLK and Coretta Scott are married.

1954
October MLK becomes pastor of the Dexter Avenue Church in Montgomery, AL.

1955
June MLK receives his Ph.D. in theology from Boston University.

December 1 Mrs. Rosa Parks refuses to give up her bus seat to a white man in Montgomery, AL.

December 5 MLK leads a year-long boycott of the Montgomery buses.

1957
January The Southern Christian Leadership Conference is founded. Dr. King is chosen president.

1959
February MLK visits India and studies Mahatma Gandhi's methods of nonviolent protest.

1960
January MLK becomes co-pastor of the Ebenezer Baptist Church with his father.

1961
May "Freedom riders" (groups of black and white people who ride buses through the South to challenge segregation) leave Washington, D.C., by bus. The bus is burned by opponents of desegregation, and the riders are beaten upon arrival in Birmingham, AL.

1963
April 12 MLK is arrested and jailed (for the thirteenth time) during a march in Birmingham, AL.

August 28 250,000 people demonstrate in Washington, D.C., for civil rights. MLK meets with President Kennedy and delivers his "I Have a Dream" speech.

November 22 President Kennedy is assassinated.

1964
December MLK is awarded the Nobel Peace Prize.

1965
The 1965 Voting Rights Act, which King sought, is signed by President Johnson.

1968
April 3 MLK delivers his last speech, "I've Been to the Mountaintop."

April 4 MLK is assassinated in Memphis, TN.

Lesson 10 — Informational Writing

Your Turn to Read the Question

Now it's your turn. Begin by reading the test question below carefully.

> Your teacher has asked you to write a report for the class about the life of Dr. Martin Luther King, Jr. Write three or more paragraphs about Dr. King's life based on the time line.
> - Make sure your first paragraph states the main idea of your report.
> - Be sure to use transitional words like *first*, *next*, and *finally*, to connect facts and events in the order in which they happened.

1. What kind of writing are you being asked to do and how do you know?

   _____

2. Who is your audience?

   _____

Your Turn to Plan

Use this sequence chart to help you answer the test question.

The Life of Dr. Martin Luther King, Jr.

Step 1

_____

_____

_____

_____

_____

_____

_____

_____

Finish Line Writing

Your Turn to Write a Draft

Now it's your turn to write a draft. Before you begin, review your graphic organizer. Think about what your main idea should be. What is it that you are going to explain? Are all the facts and events in order? Do you need to add details to explain each step better? Remember to use transitional words such as *first, next, after,* and *finally* to help your sentences flow smoothly.

_____
_____
_____
_____
_____
_____
_____
_____
_____
_____
_____
_____
_____
_____
_____
_____
_____
_____
_____

When you have finished your draft, go back over it. Make your revisions on this page. Proofread your draft. Then write your final answer on your own paper.

Your Turn to Score Writing

Use this rubric to review your own paper. Then review another student's paper. Write your suggestions for ways the paper could be improved. Give the paper a score based on this rubric.

Rubric for Informational Writing

Score 3
- The writing answers all parts of the test question.
- The ideas are well developed and organized in a way that makes sense.
- There is a clear main idea and details to support it.
- The writing is easy to read and holds the reader's attention.
- Words are used correctly and well.
- There are almost no mistakes in grammar, capitalization, punctuation, and spelling.

Score 2
- The writing answers almost all parts of the test question.
- At least a few ideas are well developed and connected to one another.
- There is a main idea and some details to support it, though they may be somewhat unclear.
- The writing mostly stays on the subject but may have some details that don't belong.
- Some words may be misused.
- There are some mistakes in grammar, capitalization, punctuation, and spelling.

Score 1
- The writing answers only part of the test question.
- The ideas don't go together well and they are not organized in a way that makes sense.
- The main idea is unclear, or there may be several main ideas.
- The writing strays from the main subject and is hard to follow.
- Many words are overused or misused.
- There are several mistakes in grammar, capitalization, punctuation, and spelling.

Lesson 11: Descriptive Writing

Sometimes your purpose in writing will be to create a vivid picture of a person, place, or thing. This type of writing is called **descriptive writing**. When writing a description, it's impossible to include every single detail about a subject. Instead you'll need to start by deciding on the feeling you would like your readers to come away with. Then choose details to make this feeling come alive.

The best way to "paint a picture" of something for a reader is to use details that relate to the senses. For example, a descriptive paragraph about a walk in a forest might include details about the smell of pine trees in the air, sunlight streaming through the trees, and the sounds of birds overhead.

In most descriptive paragraphs, a topic sentence introduces the subject and suggests a feeling about it. The supporting details that follow help to bring the subject to life. The concluding sentence sums up the overall feeling about the person, place, or thing being described.

Read the test question below.

> You have been asked to write a paragraph for younger students about one of your favorite places. Bring this place to life using details about what it looks like, sounds like, smells like, and feels like.
>
> - Be sure to use details that make the reader feel like he or she is there.
> - Arrange your details in logical order.

Reading the Question

Now you will see how one student, Nadine, approached the test question. She began by reading the test question carefully. The words *using details about what it looks like, sounds like, smells like, and feels like* gave her the clues she needed to know that she would be writing a descriptive paragraph. The words *about one of your favorite places* told her she would be writing about her own experience.

Then, she read the question once more for clues about her audience. The question reads: "You have been asked to write a paragraph for younger students. . . ." Because she would be writing for younger students, she knew her writing needed to be lively and interesting to hold their attention.

Nadine spent about three minutes reading the test question. She made sure she understood exactly what it was asking before she began planning what to write.

Planning to Write

The next step is to make a plan using a graphic organizer. In this case, Nadine knew she had to use details about what a place looks, sounds, smells, and feels like. Nadine chose a simple sensory chart to organize the details.

Prewriting

Subject: On the Roof
Sight   people and cars below
Sound   dogs barking, the hum of traffic below
Smell   air smells clean up this high
Taste
Touch/Feel   it's cool out and I shiver
Thoughts/Feelings   feels like a special treat

Sorting Sensory Details

Look at the details below and think about the senses each is related to. Label each item *sight, sound, smell, taste, touch,* or *thoughts/feelings*.

1. _____ The smell of blueberry waffles wafted through the air.

2. _____ I felt very nervous as I walked toward the door.

3. _____ The smooth fabric reminded me of silk.

4. _____ I could taste the salty air as we got closer to the beach.

5. _____ The loud crash of the dishes startled me.

Writing a Draft

Once you've developed a plan for your writing, you will be ready to write your first draft. Don't worry about making your first draft perfect. You can change things later. The important thing is to write down your ideas.

Nadine based her first draft below on the sensory chart from the previous page. Look closely at the first and last sentences of her draft. Did her first sentence introduce the subject and suggest an overall feeling about it? Did her last sentence sum up the overall feeling of the subject well?

Drafting

From the roof top garden of my apartment building, I watch the people and Cars below and feel like nothing can be wrong with the World. there is always wind here on the roof. Today it's coool out and shiver as it blows against back. The air smells clean up this high. I see a fly by and look at me—maybe wondering if we are sharng the same feeling. i'm amzed at brightly the sun light reflects of the cars passing by. i hear dog barking, and the hum of trafic below. it feels like a special treat to sit so peacefully and so high above the busy street below. The air smells clean up this high.

1. What specific event was Nadine describing? _____

2. Circle and label words that describe sights and sounds.

Revising and Proofreading

The text below shows how Nadine revised her first draft. Keep your eyes open for errors that she may have missed!

_____
(Title)

Revising

From the rooftop garden of my apartment building, I watch the people
and ~~C~~/the/cars below and feel like nothing can be wrong with the World. ~~there~~/T/ is
always wind here on the roof. Today it's coool out/,/ and /I/ shiver as ~~it~~/the wind/ blows
against /my/ back. The air smells clean up this high. I see a /bird/ fly by and look at
me—maybe wondering if we are shar/i/ng the same feeling. ~~i~~/I/'m amzed at
/how/ brightly the sun light reflects of the cars passing by. ~~i~~/I/ hear /a/ dog barking,
and the hum of tra/f/ic below. ~~it~~/I/t feels like a special treat to sit so peacefully
~~and so high~~ above the busy street below. ~~The air smells clean up this high.~~

1. Why in sentence three has *it* been replaced with "the wind?" _____

_____

2. Why did the writer cross out the last sentence? _____

_____

3. Write a title for this descriptive paragraph on the line above the draft.

4. Imagine you live in the same apartment building as Nadine. Describe the part of the rooftop garden that you would have planted. (Think about what grows in a garden: flowers, vegetables, vines, grass, shrubs.)

_____

_____

_____

Proofreading

Proofread Nadine's draft for six more errors. Write your corrections on the draft above.

Finish Line Writing

Your Turn to Read

Mrs. Arnold has put together a shopping list for Thanksgiving dinner. She'll be cooking for the whole family. Read Mrs. Arnold's list carefully. You will use details from her list to do some descriptive writing.

Thanksgiving Shopping List

- 18-lb. turkey
- 2 bags onions
- 3 packages mushrooms
- fresh cranberries
- 8 sticks butter
- bread for stuffing
- 1 lb. green beans
- 6 sweet potatoes
- 2 butternut squashes
- yeast for dough
- lettuce
- tomatoes
- cucumbers
- carrots
- brown sugar
- 5 lemons
- 4 pie crusts
- pecans (for pie)
- apples (for pie)
- 3 cans pumpkin filling (for pie)
- ice cream (chocolate, vanilla, strawberry)
- whipping cream
- chocolate topping
- coffee
- cinnamon

Lesson 11 — Descriptive Writing

Your Turn to Read the Question

Now it's your turn. Begin by reading the test question below carefully.

> Think of a real or imaginary Thanksgiving dinner. Use items from Mrs. Arnold's shopping list on the previous page to write a description telling the details of this Thanksgiving meal. What was served? How did the food smell and taste?
> - Describe the details of the meal using words related to the five senses.
> - Make sure your conclusion sums up the overall feeling of your description.

1. What kind of writing are you being asked to do, and how do you know?

_____

_____

2. What subject is the test question asking you to write about?

_____

Your Turn to Plan

Use this sensory chart to help you answer the test question.

Subject:
Sight
Sound
Smell
Taste
Touch/Feel
Thoughts/Feelings

Finish Line Writing 101

Your Turn to Write a Draft

Now it's your turn to write a draft. Before you begin, review your graphic organizer. Think about how your topic sentence will introduce the Thanksgiving dinner and the details that follow. How will supporting details make readers feel like they are there? Make sure to use interesting, lively words.

___

When you have finished your draft, go back over it. Make your revisions on this page. Proofread your draft. Then write your final answer on your own paper.

Your Turn to Score Writing

Use this rubric to review your own paper. Then review another student's paper. Write your suggestions for ways the paper could be improved. Give the paper a score based on this rubric.

Rubric for Descriptive Writing

Score 3
- The writing answers all parts of the test question.
- The supporting details appeal to the senses and draw the reader in.
- The introduction, supporting details, and concluding sentence are clear.
- The concluding sentence sums up the overall feeling of the paragraph.
- Words are used correctly and well.
- There are almost no mistakes in grammar, capitalization, punctuation, and spelling.

Score 2
- The writing answers almost all parts of the test question.
- Some of the supporting details appeal to the senses and draw the reader in.
- The introduction, supporting details, and concluding sentences are somewhat unclear.
- The concluding sentence relates to the paragraph.
- Some worlds are misused.
- There are some mistakes in grammar, capitalization, punctuation, and spelling.

Score 1
- The writing answers only part of the test question.
- The supporting details do not appeal to the senses or draw the reader in.
- The introduction, supporting details, and concluding sentences are not easy to identify.
- The concluding sentence does not relate to the paragraph.
- Many words are overused or misused.
- There are several mistakes in grammar, capitalization, punctuation, and spelling.

Lesson 12 Writing to Persuade

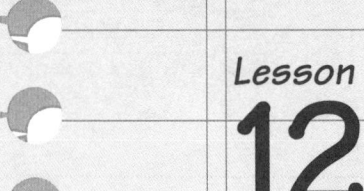

When you want to convince someone to think the way you do about a subject, you use **persuasive writing.** You can simply write your opinion, but you are more likely to persuade your reader if you present facts, examples, and reasons to support your point of view.

Persuasive writing can be a letter, an e-mail message, or a column in a magazine. Newspapers include editorials that try to persuade readers about which candidate to vote for in an election. Readers may send in letters to the editor, which are printed on the same page. You might write a letter to a city official to try to persuade him not to close a city swimming pool. Or you might send an e-mail to a friend to convince her to go to the movies with you.

You can start your persuasive writing by stating your opinion right away or by leading up to it. For most persuasive writing—especially for a test, it is a good idea to begin with your opinion. Then you must provide reasons and information to really persuade your readers. Your concluding sentence should sum up your ideas with a strong ending.

Here is a test question that requires you to do some persuasive writing.

> Your friends have asked you to write a short letter to convince your school principal that the lunch menu should be changed to include pizza every day.
> - Be sure to state your opinion clearly in the opening sentence.
> - Use facts and examples, not opinions, in your supporting sentences.
> - Arrange your supporting points in order of importance.

Reading the Question

Here is how one student, Jake, approached the test question. He began by reading the question carefully. Words in the test question like *to convince* and *state your opinion* were clues that let him know he was being asked to write a persuasive letter.

Then, he read the question once more for clues about his audience. The question reads: "Your friends have asked you to write a short letter to convince your school principal. . . ." Because he would need to write to convince someone older and more knowledgeable, Jake needed to make sure his facts were strong.

Jake spent about three minutes reading the test question. He made sure he understood exactly what it was asking before he began planning what to write.

Planning to Write

The next step is to make a plan for what you will write. It's important to choose a graphic organizer that works well for the kind of writing you need to do. In this case, the test question asks Jake to write a letter to his principal that states an opinion in the opening sentence, uses facts and examples in supporting sentences, and arranges points that support his opinion in their order of importance.

Here Jake chose to use a main opinion and fact chart to help him collect the details for his persuasive paragraph.

Prewriting

Main Opinion: For a number of reasons, I strongly believe that pizza should be available every day on the school lunch menu.
Fact 1 (Least important) The kids at school will be happier if they like something on the menu every day.
Fact 2 Most kids love pizza. They will eat lunch.
Fact 3 Pizza is not expensive to make.
Fact 4 Pizza can provide all of the food groups!
Fact 5 (Most important) Pizza can be healthy and low in fat—if it's made with things like wheat flour, low-fat cheeses and meats, and vegetables and toppings.

Finish Line Writing

Writing a Draft

Once you've developed a plan for your writing, you are ready to write your first draft. Don't worry about making your first draft perfect. You can change things later. The important thing is to write down your ideas.

This is Jake's draft based on his main opinion and fact chart.

Drafting

Dear Principal Arnold,

For a number of reasons, I strongly believe that Pizza should available every day on the school lunch menu. first of all, the kids at school will be happier. They are happy if they like something on the menu every day. Second, because most kids love pizza it's a great way way to make sure they're eating lunch. Pizza is easy and not that expensive to make. With the right ingredients, pizza can kids provide with all of the food groups! My cousin works on weekends at Poppy's Pizza.

Most important, pizza can healthy and low in Fat—if it's made using fresh, wholesome, ingredients like wheat flour, low-fat cheeses and Meats, and a variety of vegetables and toppings.

If pizza were on the school lunch menu every day the student population would be hapier and healthier. I really think pizza every day is the way to go.

Sincerly,

Jake Morelos

1. What is Jake's topic sentence? _____
2. Circle the transitional words or phrases that he uses.
3. What is his concluding sentence? Does it work well? Why or why not?

_____

_____

Revising and Proofreading

Here is how Jake revised his first draft. Read the revision and answer the questions. Keep your eyes open for errors that he may have missed!

Dear Principal Arnold,

¶ For a number of reasons, I strongly believe that ✓Pizza should be available every day on the school lunch menu. first of all, the kids at school will be happier. ~~They are happy~~ if they like something on the menu every day. Second, because most kids love pizza, it's a great way ~~way~~ to make sure they're eating lunch. In addition, Pizza is easy and not that expensive to make. With the right ingredients, pizza can (kids) provide with all of the food groups! ~~My cousin works on weekends at Poppy's Pizza.~~

Most important, pizza can healthy and low in Fat—if it's made using fresh, wholesome ingredients like wheat flour, low-fat cheeses and Meats, and a variety of vegetables and toppings.

If pizza were on the school lunch menu every day, the student population would be hapier and healthier. I really think pizza every day is the way to go.

Sincerly,

Jake Morelos

1. Which two sentences did Jake combine? _____

2. What transitional phrase did he add? _____

There are four more errors in Jake's draft. Write them on the draft above.

Finish Line Writing 107

Your Turn to Read

Read the newspaper article below. You'll use facts from this article to do some persuasive writing.

Controversial Decision to Build Amusement Park Stalled

By Deborah Chang

Fairfield town officials managed to stall another week on a decision regarding controversial plans to build Funpark. Those in favor of the new amusement park welcome the jobs and business it will bring to their sleepy little town. Since last year's closing of two local steel factories, hundreds of local workers have struggled to find work. The building of Funpark would bring 150 new jobs to Fairfield. Ferris construction now has the green light to begin building Funpark on Turner's Field, one of the most popular baseball fields in town.

Meanwhile, many parents are up in arms. Turner's Field, they say, provides local kids with the open space they need to exercise and play. Funpark, they say, will not benefit local children's welfare. They fear the amusement park will distract young people from more productive activities and bring increased traffic to town. In the words of Edward Greenfield, a local, "Without Turner's Field, my son and the 70 kids who play in the Fairfield Little League won't have a place to practice. That's not fair. Why can't they find another place to build Funpark?" Sherice Bendel, Funpark's spokeswoman responded by saying, "We believe, in time, these issues will be resolved, and Funpark will become a welcome addition to the town of Fairfield."

Your Turn to Read the Question

Now it's your turn. Begin by reading the test question below carefully.

> Imagine you live in Fairfield. What do you think about the decision to build Funpark? Write a letter to the mayor of Fairfield to convince him or her of your opinion about the issue.
> - Include an opening sentence that clearly states your overall opinion about the building of Funpark.
> - Make your supporting sentences back up your opinion with facts. Use facts from the newspaper article and from your own experience.

1. What kind of writing are you being asked to do, and how do you know?

_____

_____

2. What type of information is the test question asking you to use as facts to support your opinion?

_____

Your Turn to Plan

Use this main opinion and fact chart to help you answer the test question. Fill in as many facts as needed.

Main Opinion:
Fact 1

Finish Line Writing 109

Your Turn to Write a Draft

Now it's your turn to write a draft. Before you begin, review your graphic organizer. Make sure your opening sentence states your opinion about the Funpark issue clearly. Are your supporting details all based on facts? Make sure to use transitional words to connect your supporting points.

_____

When you have finished your draft, go back over it. Make your revisions on this page. Proofread your draft. Then write your final answer on your own paper.

Your Turn to Score Writing

Use this rubric to review your own paper. Then review another student's paper. Write your suggestions for ways the paper could be improved. Give the paper a score based on this rubric.

Rubric for Writing to Persuade

Score 3
- The writing answers all parts of the test question.
- The supporting details use facts, not opinions, to convince readers.
- The introduction, supporting details, and concluding sentence are clear.
- The concluding sentence sums up the overall opinion and adds a strong ending.
- Words are used correctly and well.
- There are almost no mistakes in grammar, capitalization, punctuation, and spelling.

Score 2
- The writing answers almost all parts of the test question.
- Some of the supporting details use facts to convince readers.
- The introduction, supporting details, and concluding sentence are somewhat unclear.
- The concluding sentence relates to the preceding sentences.
- Some words are misused.
- There are some mistakes in grammar, capitalization, punctuation, and spelling.

Score 1
- The writing answers only part of the test question.
- The supporting details do not use facts to convince readers.
- The introduction, supporting details, and concluding sentence are not easy to identify.
- The concluding sentence does not relate to the preceding sentences.
- Many words are overused or misused.
- There are several mistakes in grammar, capitalization, punctuation, and spelling.

Lesson 13 Writing Sentences

Writing is a way to share ideas and to communicate with others. Whether you are writing an e-mail to a friend or a report for school, you want to get your message across. The words you choose and the sentences you write can make your meaning clear—or they can give the wrong message.

The best writing is easy to read and uses specific details and words. You can tell your friend that a movie was "really funny," but your friend will know just how funny if you say you're "still laughing about the last scene." You can say that your mom's spaghetti is good, or you can tell her it's flavorful, delicious, and scrumptious.

Verbs

Start improving your written sentences by looking at the verbs you use. Are they specific, or do you use the most common verb you can think of? Look at the following sentence. What other verbs could be used in place of *jumped*?

 Suddenly, the horse jumped over the wall.

The word *suddenly* gives you a hint. It tells you that the horse moved quickly and unexpectedly. The horse might have *bolted, leaped, bounded,* or even *crashed*. Each verb provides a different picture of how the horse jumped.

A. In each sentence, replace the underlined verb with one that is more specific. Write your word on the line after the sentence.

1. We walked along the beach. _____
2. The fifth grade students showed their drawings. _____
3. The airplane moved down the runway. _____
4. Softly, the wind moved the leaves. _____
5. The forest fire lasted for hours. _____
6. The players ran after the soccer ball. _____
7. The moving van went down the hill. _____
8. Everyone left the building when the fire alarm rang. _____

Adjectives

Adjectives are words that describe nouns or pronouns. The more specific your adjectives are, the better your writing will be. In each example below, the adjective is in bold type, and the noun it describes is underlined.

Adjective Suddenly, the **wild** <u>horses</u> ran across the stream.

When two adjectives describe a noun, use a comma or the word *and* to separate them.

Adjectives Then the **wild, beautiful** <u>horses</u> galloped away.
Adjectives Then the **wild and beautiful** <u>horses</u> galloped away.

A. In each sentence, replace the underlined adjective with a more specific adjective or adjective phrase. You can change the order of the words. Write your new sentence on the line.

1. A hurricane is a <u>big</u> storm.

   _____

2. The <u>tired</u> hikers set up their tent at sunset.

   _____

3. The <u>tall</u> oak tree provides lots of shade.

   _____

4. We put the <u>pretty</u> flowers on the table.

   _____

5. Some football games draw <u>big, noisy</u> crowds.

   _____

B. Use specific adjectives to complete each sentence.

1. The _____ horses grazed on the prairie beneath the _____ sky.

2. Visiting the _____ building was a(n) _____ adventure for the family.

3. The _____ drizzle kept the _____ children in the house all day.

Finish Line Writing 113

Adverbs

Adverbs are words that describe or tell about verbs, adjectives, or other adverbs. Many adverbs end in *ly*. Adverbs can come before or after the word they modify or tell about.

Adverbs tell *when, where, how, to what extent,* and *how often*. In each example below, the adverb is in bold type, and the word that it describes is underlined.

Describes a Verb Jack <u>answered</u> the phone **quickly.**
Describes an Adjective We were **extremely** <u>proud</u> of Marty.
Describes an Adverb That track star runs **very** <u>fast</u>.

When	Where	How, To What Extent, How Often
go **soon**	fly **overhead**	walks **rapidly**
eat **later**	zoom **around**	**completely** revises
arrive **early**	look **everywhere**	jogs **frequently**

Just like choosing an adjective, the more specific the adverb you choose, the more descriptive your writing will be.

A. In each sentence, replace the underlined adverb with one that is more specific. Write your word on the line after the sentence.

1. Do you see that <u>really</u> large cloud? _____
2. <u>Later</u>, it will be moving in our direction. _____
3. The storm is <u>quickly</u> increasing in intensity. _____
4. A deadly tornado can pack <u>very</u> high winds. _____
5. If there is a tornado nearby, find shelter <u>soon</u>! _____

B. Use an adverb to complete each sentence.

1. The kitchen light burns more _____ than the others.
2. Janice _____ recognized her mistake.
3. Walk _____ when crossing the street.
4. The _____ colorful balloons arrived just as the crowd sang "Happy Birthday."
5. Speak _____ so that everyone can _____ understand you.

Lesson 13 — Writing Sentences

Revising Sentences

After you write a draft of a paragraph or essay, you go back to revise it for content and structure. You can revise your sentences at that time, too. You can replace weak or overused words in a sentence, or you can revise the whole sentence to make details clear.

Suppose you start with this sentence:

We saw a cute little chimpanzee slowly peel a banana and eat it up.

You can change some of the words this way:

We watched a young chimpanzee carefully peel a banana and gobble it up.

You can also incorporate details:

We watched a young chimpanzee gently peel a banana then toss the peel away and devour the fruit in two bites.

A. On the line below each sentence, write a new sentence on the same topic using more specific and stronger words.

1. The weather was awesome for our family picnic.

   _____

2. We all had so much fun.

   _____

3. Even Grandma Carter was there, and she looked good.

   _____

4. Uncle Mitch looked extra happy.

   _____

5. We definitely had a terrific turnout.

   _____

6. At the end of the day, everyone was really, really tired.

   _____

7. We did a lot of great stuff and ate a lot of great food, too.

   _____

8. We all said it was the best picnic ever.

   _____

Sentence Length

When you are revising a draft, look at the length of your sentences. If most of your sentences are long or short, think about changing them. Too many short sentences will make your writing sound choppy. Too many long sentences may sound dull. Here are some ways to vary the length of the sentences in your writing.

Compound Sentences

A compound sentence is two simple sentences joined by a comma and a connecting word such as *and, or,* or *but.*

Two Sentences   Eating a balanced diet is important. Even fast-food restaurants have some healthy food choices now.

Compound Sentence   Eating a balanced diet is important, **and** even fast food restaurants have some healthy food choices now.

Two Sentences   Dad backed the car down the driveway. He had to wait for traffic to clear.

Compound Sentence   Dad backed the car down the driveway, **but** he had to wait for traffic to clear.

A. Combine each pair of sentences into one compound sentence. Then write the compound sentence on the line below.

1. The thunder was very loud. Lightning lit up the night sky.

   _____

2. Rasheed will buy the quart of milk. I will stop at the vegetable stand.

   _____

3. You can buy the present today. Joan will get it tomorrow.

   _____

4. Luke finished his homework early. He still couldn't go to the basketball game.

   _____

5. Jack will make the meatballs. You can make the sauce.

   _____

6. Erin sent me an invitation. I cannot be there that early.

   _____

Lesson 13 — Writing Sentences

Compound Subjects and Compound Predicates

If two sentences with different subjects have the same predicate, you can combine the sentences. Just write one sentence with a **compound subject.** Here each subject is underlined once, and each predicate is underlined twice.

I waited in line to buy tickets. My three friends waited in line, too.

My three friends and I waited in line to buy tickets.

If two sentences with different predicates have the same subject, you can combine the sentences. Just write one sentence with a compound predicates.

The bird landed on the tree branch. It looked around.

The bird landed on the tree branch and looked around.

B. Combine each pair of sentences into one sentence. Then write the new sentence on the line provided.

1. Once aboard, we raised the sail. We pulled up the anchor.

   _____

2. We had tickets to the concert. We went Saturday night.

   _____

3. Members can go to the museum for free. Students can, too.

   _____

4. Jean wanted to go to the library. Her brothers also wanted to go.

   _____

5. Tony called us tonight. He asked for directions.

   _____

6. Oil is a fossil fuel. Coal and natural gas are fossil fuels.

   _____

7. My mother grew up in Boston. Her father also grew up in Boston.

   _____

8. The swimmer put on her cap. She dove into the pool.

   _____

Finish Line Writing

Prepositional Phrases

A **prepositional phrase** is a group of words that begins with a preposition and ends with its object, which is a noun. A prepositional phrase may also include words that describe its object.

Compare the following prepositional phrases. In each phrase the preposition is in bold type and its object is underlined. Notice the words used to describe the object in the second example for each phrase.

Prepositional   **in** the park   **in** the city's new park
Phrases   **up** a tree   **up** a large oak tree

Sometimes you can combine two sentences by changing one of them into a prepositional phrase. Then you can add the phrase to the sentence that comes either before or after it.

> The troop camped out overnight. They camped **in the park.**
> The troop camped out overnight **in the park.**

C. Combine each pair of sentences into one sentence.

1. I spotted the frog. It was at the other end of the pond.

   _____

2. My mother is starting a new job. She will start in the fall.

   _____

3. Her family lives in a log cabin. It is in the woods.

   _____

4. Oliver went mountain climbing last summer. He went to the state park.

   _____

5. Jennifer likes to work in the garden. She likes to garden on Saturdays.

   _____

6. They left in the morning. It was before dawn.

   _____

7. I had a report due at school today. It was about polar bears.

   _____

Varying Sentence Length

Now that you have learned some ways to vary length of sentences in your writing, do the following exercise.

A. Rewrite each item below. Vary the length of the sentences to improve the writing.

1. Hannah went into the grocery store on the corner, and she saw Shelby. They talked for a while, but Shelby had to leave. She had a music lesson, and she didn't want to be late.

2. Hector can run fast. Hector can hit well. Hector can pitch a fastball.

3. More than 2,000 years ago, the Greeks living in a part of Turkey called Magnesia discovered an unusual rock that attracted materials that contained iron so the Greeks named it magnetite.

4. Gerbils make good pets. Cats make good pets. They don't get along well with one another.

5. During our class trip to Washington, D.C., I learned a lot. I learned a lot about our government.

Finish Line Writing 119

Revising for Effective Writing

Read the following essay. Then revise each paragraph for word choice, sentence length, and the other elements of good writing, and make your revisions below. Write the revised essay on a separate piece of paper.

> We had a frost last night. It happened late. The temperature dropped real low. It was about 27 degrees. This is just totally incredible because we almost never gets a frost in Miami, Florida. The flowers on our street were hit really, really hard. Some turned brown. Some withered. It was so bad for them. People on my street said they has seen this happen in the past, but not very often.
>
> Me and my friends woke up to this sight, and it was very sad seeing the damaged flowers and we were really concerned about the farmers and their crops. A frost like this can cost lots of people lots of money. The oranges do not ripen. The grapefruits do not ripen. Neither the farmer nor his customers gets what they need.

Putting It All Together

Read the paragraphs below. Using what you have learned in the sentence lessons, edit the paragraphs to correct sentence fragments and run-on sentences, capitalization, punctuation, subject-verb agreement and other errors. Make your edits right on the paragraphs.

We went to maine on our summer vacation. It was great I had a lot of fun. There was a lot to do. We slept in a tent in a campground. The campground was right on the water. very pretty. The ocean waves were very relaxing. The ocean waves helped me fall asleep each night.

there was some other kids at the campground too and we had fun me and them built sandcastles on the beach. Tidal pools formed farther down the beach. We saw sea anemones sea urchins crabs and small fish. They were wriggling around it was funny to watch them.

One day we went. hiking in the woods and we saw a deer and wild turkey. Turkeys are really funny looking. Me and my father took pictures of the animals. A park ranger guided our hike and she told us about all the different types of trees and other vegetation in the woods and she told us that there were pine trees in the woods that were hundreds of years old!

On our last night, we walked along the beech. As the sun were setting. Ribbons of color began to form in the evening sky I had a really good time on our summer vacation.

Test-Taking Tips

You are about to take a writing test. Before you begin, review these tips for taking a test.

Prepare ahead of time.
- Bring more than one pen or pencil. Be sure they work!
- Get plenty of sleep the night before.
- Eat a good breakfast on the morning of the test.

Budget your time.
- Spend most of your time on planning and drafting.
- Make a schedule based on the time available. For example, if you have one hour, figure 5 minutes for reading the question, 10 minutes for planning, 30 minutes for drafting, and 15 minutes for revising and proofreading.
- Check the clock during the test. Are you on schedule?

Stick to the question.
- Make sure you know what the question asks you to do.
- Read the question carefully. Underline it or make notes on it. Go over it as many times as necessary to be sure you get it.
- After you plan, go back and read the question again. Ask yourself if your plan will result in a complete answer to the question.
- Before you revise, ask yourself, "Did I answer all parts of the test question?"

Relax.
- Don't race or skip over any part of the process, such as reading the question carefully or revising and proofreading.
- Remember that you have practiced all of this before. You are ready!
- Remember that you have learned strategies for doing your best. They are going to help you now.

Practice Test ✓

Read this passage. Then answer the questions that follow.

Firefighters to the Rescue

Firefighters perform some of the most important work in a community. They put out fires and perform many kinds of rescues. Often, they respond to medical emergencies. When someone in your town or city pulls an alarm or calls 911, chances are good that a firefighter will race to the scene.

There are many kinds of firefighting jobs. Not all of them involve fighting fires. Some firefighters teach members of their community about fire safety. Others investigate the causes of fires. They collect evidence from fires, interview witnesses, and write reports. Some firefighters work mainly as fire inspectors. They make sure buildings are safely built according to laws. Their work helps prevent fires.

Many firefighters do their jobs for free. Volunteer firefighters rush to work when an alarm is called in. They also spend some of their free time training, maintaining equipment, and doing other needed chores. Some firefighters are paid for full-time work. When they are not at the scene of a fire, they do other work in the community or at the firehouse. They may also be learning about new methods for fighting and preventing fires. Finally, some firefighters work on a "needs" basis. They go to a fire when they are called, and they are paid only for that work. Many people who fight forest fires work this way. This is especially common during summers, when most forest fires occur.

Fighting a fire requires many different personality traits. One of the most important is the ability to think fast. A person has to respond quickly to an alarm. When a fire breaks out, there is often not a minute to lose. The unique problems of each emergency can require different solutions. A firefighter should also be in good physical shape. Quick thinking and quick action often go together.

Firefighters need specialized knowledge and training. They have to become familiar with all the equipment and learn to use it well. For example, they have to use equipment ranging from tower ladders to safety lines. They have to understand how pumper trucks and high-pressure hoses work. They have to develop knowledge of different causes and kinds of fires.

At the scene of a fire, firefighters have to stay calm. They must think and act under pressure. A firefighter may have only a few moments to save

Go On

someone trapped in a building. In such a situation, a roof could collapse. Walls could cave in. Smoke could become deadly.

A firefighter also has to have excellent people skills. Firefighters have to know how to get terrified people to trust them. A firefighter also has to work well as a member of a team.

Some firefighters take great risks to help save people and property. At times, they are injured, often from smoke. Some pay the ultimate price. Still, firefighters go bravely forward to do their job no matter what the risk.

Short-Response Questions

Use the information from the passage to answer each of the following questions in two or three sentences.

1. What are three traits that a firefighter should have?

2. What are three different jobs that firefighters do?

Read the Question and Plan

Read this test question. You may underline it or mark it up as you wish.

> Firefighters are important members of a community. The work they do saves people, pets, homes, and other property. Do you think you have what it takes to be a firefighter? If so, what kind of firefighting job or role would you want? Write an essay stating your opinion about firefighting as a possible career or volunteer activity. Your response should include at least three paragraphs.
>
> In your response be sure to
> - state your opinion
> - support your opinion with three or more facts or reasons
> - fully explain each fact or reason

Use the rest of this page to plan your response. Choose a graphic organizer to arrange your ideas.

Write Your Draft

Use this page to write your draft.

After you revise and proofread your draft, write your response on a separate piece of paper.

Editing

Here is an essay that one student wrote about her neighbor, a volunteer firefighter. Proofread this paper for mistakes. Write your corrections on the essay using standard proofreading marks.

My neighbor abigail Levy has been a volunteer firefighter in our town since 1991. Wanting to be a good member of her community. She first thought about volunteering in her son's elementary school. Than one of her friends told her that Springfield needed more volunteer firefighters. So, she went to see what it was all about.

Ms. Levy learned that, in springfield, firefighters get called more often for medical problems than for fires. They fight fires, too but often more they go out because someone is injured or having a heart attack. At first, Ms. Levy didn't know if she wanted to join or not. The firefighters said she should try out the training coarse. It was at their fire academy and then decide.

Ms. Levy did the ten-week course. She learned about fire safety. She learned about fire equipment. She learned many rescue techniques. Read hundreds of pages! She also had to do a lot of exercises that she still does now. After she passed the course, she decided to serve her community. She decided to serve as a firefighter. Ms Levy says she also likes having a car with a flashing red light on top!

Handbook

Capitalization

- Capitalize the first word of a sentence.

    The sun is shining.

- Capitalize names and initials of people.

    Tracy G. Peters   Uncle Henry   Mayor Soto

- Capitalize people's titles when they are used as part of the name.

    Ms. Courtney Evans   S. Jenkins, Jr.

- Capitalize the names of days, months, places, and holidays.

Days	Months	Places	Holidays
Wednesday	April	Brook Hill Middle School	Valentine's Day
Friday	June	Arizona	Memorial Day
Monday	November	Washington, D.C.	Thanksgiving

- Do NOT capitalize the names of the seasons.

    winter, fall, spring, summer

Punctuation

End Marks

- A statement ends with a period: Pine trees stay green all year.

- A question ends with a question mark: Did you finish your math?

- An exclamation ends with an exclamation point: What a great movie!

Commas

- Use a comma between the parts of a compound sentence. Place the comma before the word *and, but,* or *or*.

    A cold wind whistled, **but** the cabin remained warm and cozy.

- Use commas between words or phrases in a series.

    We packed tuna sandwiches, pickles, and apple juice.

- Use a comma between the day and year in a date: February 11, 2006

- Use a comma between a city and state: Memphis, Tennessee

Apostrophes

- Make a singular noun possessive by adding an apostrophe and -s.

    the boss**'s** desk   a child**'s** toy

- When a plural noun ends in s, make it possessive by adding just an apostrophe. When a plural noun does not end in s, make it possessive by adding an apostrophe and -s.

    two students**'** reports   children**'s** books

- Use an apostrophe to show where letters are missing in a contraction:

    has + not = hasn**'**t (*o* is missing)   I + am = I**'**m (*a* is missing)

Quotation Marks

- Use quotation marks before and after a person's exact words.

    Sam said, "Anya forgot her lunch."

Titles

- Capitalize the first word, last word, and every important word in a title. Use quotation marks for titles of short works.

    article: "How to Make a Kite"
    short story: "The Lion and the Mouse"
    poem: "A Cat"

Underline or use italics for longer works.

book: <u>Shiloh</u> or *Shiloh*
newspaper: <u>The Boston Globe</u> or *The Boston Globe*

Grammar and Usage

Subject-Verb Agreement

- When you use an action verb in the present tense, add the ending -s or -es to the verb if the subject is a singular noun or a singular pronoun (but not if the subject is either *I* or *you*).

    she swims   Amy swims

- Do not add -s or -es to the verb if the subject is plural, *I*, or *you*.

    Amy and Lori swim   the girls swim   I swim   you swim

Finish Line Writing

Subject-Verb Agreement with Forms of *be*

- With a singular noun subject, use *is* for the present tense and *was* for the past tense.

    Charles **is** here.   The weather **was** sunny last weekend.

- With a plural noun or a compound subject, use *are* for the present tense and *were* for the past tense.

    The students **are** late.   Luis and Eric **were** at the game yesterday.

- Use the correct form of *be* with a singular or plural pronoun subject.

Present Tense		Past Tense	
Singular	Plural	Singular	Plural
I **am**	we **are**	I **was**	we **were**
you **are**	you **are**	you **were**	you **were**
he, she, *or* it **is**	they **are**	he, she, *or* it **was**	they **were**

Irregular Verbs

The verbs below and many others are called irregular because their past-tense forms do not end in *ed*. Use the correct past-tense forms of irregular verbs.

Present	Past	Past Participle
is	was	(has) been
begin	began	(has) begun
bring	brought	(has) brought
choose	chose	(has) chosen
come	came	(has) come
fly	flew	(has) flown
go	went	(has) gone
have	had	(has) had
know	knew	(has) known
make	made	(has) made
run	ran	(has) run
say	said	(has) said
speak	spoke	(has) spoken
swim	swam	(has) swum
take	took	(has) taken
wear	wore	(has) worn
write	wrote	(has) written

Subject and Object Pronouns

Pronouns have different subject and object forms. Use the subject form as the subject of a sentence. Use the object form after an action verb or after a preposition such as *of, to, for,* or *about*. The pronouns *you* and *it* have only one form.

Subject Pronouns	
Singular	Plural
I	we
he	they
she	

Object Pronouns	
Singular	Plural
me	us
him	them
her	

Wrong: Sara and **me** are here.
Correct: Sara and **I** are here.

Wrong: Ann told Gina and **I**.
Correct: Ann told Gina and **me**.

Wrong: Don and **her** like chess.
Correct: Don and **she** like chess.

Wrong: Give the pens to **he** and **I**.
Correct: Give the pens to **him** and **me**.

Naming Yourself Last

When you speak of yourself and another person, name yourself (I or me) last.

Roger and I are neighbors.   Grandpa wrote to **Simon** and **me**.

Possessive Pronouns

Use these possessive pronouns before a noun to show ownership.

Singular	Plural
my	our
your	your
his, her, its	their

Someone took **her** and **my** seats.

Use these possessive pronouns when a noun does not follow.

Singular	Plural
mine	ours
yours	yours
his, hers, its	theirs

These seats are **hers** and **mine**.

Tricky Words

Some words are often confused. Remember to use these words correctly.

a/an	Use *a* before a consonant sound. Use *an* before a vowel sound. Wrong: **a** orange Correct: **an** orange

can/may	In a question, use *can* to ask if something is possible. Use *may* to ask if something is allowed.
	    Wrong: **Can** I borrow your pen?
	    Correct: **May** I borrow your pen?

good/well	Use *good* only as an adjective. Use *well* as an adverb unless you are describing someone's state of health.
	    Wrong: He pitches **good**.
	    Correct: He pitches **well**. He is a **good** pitcher.
	    Wrong: I have a cold and don't feel **good**.
	    Correct: I have a cold and don't feel **well**.

have/of	Use *have* or *'ve* after words such as *could*, *should*, and *would*. Do not use *of*.
	    Wrong: I could **of** gone.
	    Correct: I could **have** gone. I could**'ve** gone.

hear/here	*Hear* means "to be aware of sound": I **hear** music. (*Hear* contains *ear*!) *Here* means "in this place": Put your bags **here**.
its/it's	*Its* means "belonging to it": The dog wagged **its** tail. *It's* means "it is": **It's** raining.
than/then	*Than* is a word for comparing: Today is hotter **than** yesterday. *Then* means "at that time" or "next": Raise one arm and **then** the other.
their/there/they're	*Their* means "belonging to them": They ate **their** dinner. *There* means "in that place": **There** you are! Sit over **there**. *They're* means "they are": **They're** the fastest runners.

to/too/two	*To* means "toward" or "for the purpose of":
	    Go **to** the park **to** play.
	To can also be part of a verb form: She likes **to** skate.
	Too means "more than enough" or "also":
	    I ate **too** much. You did, **too**.
	Two means "the sum of 1 + 1": The cat had **two** kittens.

who's/whose	*Who's* means "who is": **Who's** coming to the party? *Whose* is the possessive form of *who*: I don't know **whose** hat this is.
your/you're	*Your* means "belonging to you": Put on **your** jacket. *You're* means "you are": **You're** late for the bus.

Handbook